The Errancy

ALSO BY JORIE GRAHAM

Hybrids of Plants and of Ghosts
Erosion
The End of Beauty
Region of Unlikeness
Materialism
The Best of American Poetry 1990, EDITOR
The Dream of the Unfield Field: Selected Poems 1974-1994
Earth Took of Earth: 100 Great Poems of the English
Language, EDITOR
Poems and Photographs (with JEANETTE MONTGOMERY BARRON)
Swarm

The Errancy

Poems by

JORIE GRAHAM

An Imprint of HarperCollinsPublishers

Printed in the United States of America. No part of this book
may be used or reproduced in any manner whatsoever with-
out written permission except in the case of brief quotations
embodied in critical articles and reviews. For information
address HarperCollins Publishers Inc., 10 East 53rd Street,
New York, NY 10022.

HarperCollins books may be purchased for educational,
business, or sales promotional use. For information please
write: Special Markets Department, HarperCollins Publishers
Inc., 10 East 53rd Street, New York, NY 10022.

LIBRARY OF CONGRESS CATALOGING-IN-PUBLICATION DATA

Graham, Jorie, 1950–
    The errancy / by Jorie Graham.
      p.   cm.
    ISBN 0-88001-528-4
    ISBN 0-88001-529-2 (paperback)
    I. Title.
    PS3557.R214E74   1997
    811'.54—dc20   96-44626

Designed by Susanna Gilbert, The Typeworks

The text of this book is set in Bembo

02 03 04 05 06 RRD 10 9 8 7 6 5 4 3 2

FIRST PAPERBACK EDITION 1998

Since in a net I seek to hold the wind
(Wyatt)

CONTENTS

ACKNOWLEDGMENTS

Grateful acknowledgment to the editors of the following publications in which these poems, sometimes in a different form, first appeared: *The New Yorker, Antaeus, The Paris Review, Volt, Poetry Ireland, Sulfur, New American Writing, Ploughshares, The New Republic, The American Poetry Review, Parnassus, The Iowa Review, The Denver Quarterly, The Seneca Review, The Yale Review, The Boston Review, Chants, The Kenyon Review, The Oxford Review, The New York Review of Books, Poetry Society (U.K.), P.N. Review (U.K.), The London Review of Books.*

The Errancy

The Guardian Angel of the Little Utopia

Shall I move the flowers again?
Shall I put them further to the left
into the light?
Will that fix it, will that arrange the
thing?
Yellow sky.
Faint cricket in the dried-out bush.
As I approach, my footfall in the leaves
drowns out the cricket-chirping I was
coming close to hear . . .
Yellow sky with black leaves rearranging it.
Wind rearranging the black leaves in it.
But anyway I am indoors, of course, and this is a pane, here,
and I have arranged the flowers for you
again. Have taken the dead cordless ones, the yellow bits past apogee,
the faded cloth, the pollen-free abandoned marriage-hymn
back out, leaving the few crisp blooms to swagger, winglets, limpid
                                        debris. . . .
Shall I arrange these few remaining flowers?
Shall I rearrange these gossamer efficiencies?
Please don't touch me with your skin.
Please let the thing evaporate.
Please tell me clearly what it is.
The party is so loud downstairs, bristling with souvenirs.
It's a philosophy of life, of course,
drinks fluorescent, whips of syntax in the air
above the heads — how small they seem from here,
the bobbing universal heads, stuffing the void with eloquence,
and also tiny merciless darts
of truth. It's pulled on tight, the air they breathe and rip.
It's like a prize the way it's stretched on tight

over the voices, keeping them intermingling, forcing the breaths to

marry, marry,

cunning little hermeneutic cupola,
dome of occasion in which the thoughts re-
group, the footprints stall and gnaw in tiny ruts,
the napkins wave, are waved, the honeycombing
thoughts are felt to *dialogue,* a form of self-
congratulation, no?, or is it suffering? I'm a bit
dizzy up here rearranging things,
they will come up here soon, and need a setting for their fears,
and loves, an architecture for their evolutionary
morphic needs – what will they *need* if I don't make the place? –
what will they know to miss?, what cry out for, what feel the bitter

restless irritations

for? A bit dizzy from the altitude of everlastingness,
the tireless altitudes of the created place,
in which to make a life – a *liberty* – the hollow, fetishized, and starry

place,

a bit gossamer with dream, a vortex of evaporations,
oh little dream, invisible city, invisible hill
I make here on the upper floors for you –
down there, where you are entertained, where you are passing
time, there's glass and moss on air,
there's the feeling of being numerous, mouths submitting to air, lips

to protocol,

and dreams of sense, tongues, hinges, forceps clicking
in anticipation of . . . as if the moment, freeze-burned by accuracies-of
could be thawed open into life again
by gladnesses, by rectitude – no, no – by the sinewy efforts at
sincerity – can't you feel it gliding round you,
mutating, yielding the effort-filled phrases of your talk to air,
compounding, stemming them, honeying-open the sheerest

innuendoes till

the rightness seems to root, in the air, in the compact indoor sky,
and the rest, all round, feels like desert, falls away,
and you have the sensation of muscular timeliness,

and you feel the calligraphic in you reach out like a soul
into the midst of others, in conversation,
gloved by desire, into the tiny carnage
of opinions. . . . So dizzy. Life buzzing beneath me
though my feeling says the hive is gone, queen gone,
the continuum continuing beneath, busy, earnest, in con-
versation. Shall I prepare. Shall I put this further
to the left, shall I move the light, the point-of-view, the shades are
drawn, to cast a glow resembling disappearance, slightly red,
will that fix it, will that make clear the task, the trellised ongoingness
and all these tiny purposes, these parables, this marketplace
of tightening truths?
Oh knit me that am crumpled dust,
the heap is all dispersed. Knit me that *am*. Say *therefore*. Say
philosophy and mean by that the pane.
Let us look out again. The yellow sky.
With black leaves rearranging it. . . .

The Errancy

Then the cicadas again like kindling that won't take.
The struck match of some utopia we no longer remember
                              the terms of –
the rules. What was it was going to be abolished, what
restored? Behind them the foghorn in the harbor,
the hoarse announcements of unhurried arrivals,
the spidery virgin-shrieks of gulls, a sideways sound, a slippery
                                        utterly ash-free
delinquency
and then the subaqueous pasturings   inexhaustible
phosphorous handwritings the frothings of their own excitements now
erase, depth wrestling with the current-corridors of depth . . .
But here, up on the hill, in town,
the clusterings of dwellings in balconied crystal-formation,
the cadaverous swallowings of the dream of reason gone,
hot fingerprints where thoughts laid out these streets, these braceletings
of park and government – a hospital – a dirt-bike run –
here, we stand in our hysteria with our hands in our pockets,
quiet, at the end of day, looking out, theories stationary,
while the freight, the crazy wick, once more slides down –
marionette-like its being lowered in –
marionette-strung our outwaiting its bloody translation . . .
Utopia: remember the sensation of *direction* we loved,
how it tunneled forwardly for us,
and us so feudal in its wake –
speckling of diamond-dust as I think of it now,
that being carried forward by the notion of human
perfectibility – like a pasture imposed
on the rising vibrancy of endless diamond-dust . . .
And how we would comply, some day. How we were *built* to fit and
                                        comply –
as handwriting fits to the form of its passion,

no, to the form of its passionate bearer's fingerprintable i.d.,
or, no, to the handkerchief she brings now to her haunted face,
lifting the sunglasses to wipe away
the theory – or is it the tears? – the freight now all
in her right hand, in the oceanic place we'd pull up
through her wrist – we'd siphon right up –
marionette with her leavening of mother-of-pearl –
how she wants to be legible, how the light streaking her shades now
                                                    grows vermilion,
which she would *capture* of course, because that, she has heard,
from the rumorous diamond-dust, is what is required,
as also her spirit – now that it has been swallowed
like a lustrous hailstone by her unquenchable body – suggests – the zero
at the heart of the christened bonfire – oh little grimace, kiss, solo
at the heart – growing refined, tiny missionary, in your brightskirted
                                                    host,
scorched comprehension – because that *is* what's required,
her *putting down* now the sunset onto that page,
as an expression of her deepest undertowing sentiment,
which spidery gestures, tongued-over the molecular whiteness,
squared out and stretched and made to resemble emptiness,
will take down the smoldering in the terms of her passion
– sunglasses on the table, telephone ringing –
and be carried across the tongue-tied ocean,
through dusk, right through it, over prisons, over tiny clapboard houses
to which the bartender returns, exhausted, after work,
over flare-ups of civil strife, skeletons rotting in the arms of
skeletons, the foliage all round them gleaming,
the green belly-up god we thought we'd seen the last of,
shuddering his sleep off, first fruit hanging ripe – oh bright red zero –
right there within reach, that he too may be nourished,
you know this of course, what has awakened which we thought we'd
                                                    extinguished,
us still standing here sword in hand, hand extended,
frail, over the limpid surface of the lake-like page,
the sleep-like page, now folded and gently driven into

its envelope, for the tiny journey, over offices, over sacrifices,
to its particular address, at the heart of the metropolis,
where someone else is waiting, hailstone at the core,
and the heat is too great, friend, the passion in its envelope,
doors slamming, traffic backing-up, the populace not really
abandoned, not really, just very tired on its long red errancy
down the freeways in the dusklight
towards the little town on the hill – the *crystal-formation?* –
how long ago was it we said that? do you remember? –
and now that you've remembered – and the distance we've
traveled – and where we were, then – and
how little we've found – aren't we tired? aren't we
going to close the elaborate folder
which holds the papers in their cocoon of possibility,
the folder so pretty with its massive rose-blooms,
oh perpetual bloom, dread fatigue, and drowsiness like leavening I
feel –

The Scanning

I .

After the rain there was traffic behind us like a long kiss.
The ramp harrowing its mathematics like a newcomer who likes
                                              the rules –
glint and whir of piloting minds, gripped steering-wheels . . .
Jacob waiting and the angel *didn't show.*
Meanwhile the stations the scanner glides over, not selecting, hiss –
islands the heat-seekers missed
in the large sea of. . . . And after lunch
the long-distance starts up pianissimo – wires glinting where the
                                              frontage road
parallels the interstate for a little, narrow, while.
Elsewhere, from the air, something *softens* the scape –
which activity precedes, though doesn't necessarily require,
the carpet-bombing that often follows –
And the bands of our listening scan
the bands of static,
seeking a resting point, asymptotic, listening in the hiss
for the hoarse snagged points where meaning seemingly
accrues: three notes: three silences: intake
of breath: turnstile?: a glint in fog?: what the listener
will wait-into, hoping for a place to
stop . . . Jacob waited and the angel didn't –

2 .

Once off the interstate, we exhausted the tangible.
The plan seemed to dagger forward on its own, towards the horizon-line,
the future its mother-of-pearl cadaver, down there, where the map
                                              continues

onto the next blue page. . . . *Our* plan.
One must not pretend one knew nothing of it.
One must not pretend one didn't tenderly finger its heavenly style.
The skyline itself, bluing now towards evening,
the spidery picture of the plan we tongued up –
unquenchable – where were you? – never-to-be-defined,
a solo first-fruit performance for which the eye
is still intended. . . . What shall we move with
now that the eye must shut? What shall we sift with
now that the mind must blur? What shall we undress the veilings of
                                                    dusk with,
what shall we harvest the nothingness with,
now that the hands must be tucked back in their pockets,
now that the bright shirt of the over-ripe heart
must be taken off and the skin of things restored,
the long-haul restored (where the quicknesses had reigned),
the carpenter arriving as if out of the skyways
with a measure in hand, a sad eye, a vague patience –
the tongue-tied carpenter ready to scribble and strengthen . . .
Our plan . . . To get the beauty of it hot.
The angel called out but Jacob, Jacob . . .

                                3 .

Down by the riverbed I found some geese asleep.
I could see the billboards, but they were across the water.
Maybe two hundred geese – now beginning to stir,
purring and cooing at my walking among them.
Groping their armless way, their underneaths greening.
A slow roiling. As of redundancy. Squirming as they sponge
over the short wet grass – bunchy – the river behind presenting
                                lapidary
                                faithfulness – *plink* –
no common motion in the turbaned brooding,
all shoulder and waddle,

foliage darkening to feathers above their vague iridescence . . .
A mess of geese. Unperfectable. A mess
of conflicting notions. Something that doesn't have to be
imagined. An end-zone one can have pushed forward to,
here at the end of the path, what the whole freeway led to,
what the whole adventure led to,
galleys, slaves, log-books,
tiny calculations once it got dark enough to see,
what the whole madness led to – the curiosity – viral – here,
like a sign – thick but clear – here at the bottom of the sedge,
the city still glimmering over there in the distance,
but us here, for no reason, where the mass of geese are rousing,
necessity and circumstance quivering in each other's arms,
us in each other's arms, or, no, not really.

4 .

The angel was on the telephone.
No, Jacob was on the telephone.
There was no doorway through which to pass.
For either of them. No flaming gateway. No wafer-thin scribble
to *understand*. . . .
Was it really, then, a pastime, the hostile universe?
Was the wrestling a mental color, an architecture of mockery,
a self-portrait of the unmargined thing by the margined thing?
The geese seemed to assemble, the freeway hissed.
Oh to sleep the sleep of those who are alive. . . .
The brain extended its sugared fingertips.
Itching so to create something new.
Slightly, profoundly, the riverbottom gleamed.

5 .

Then *here,* and *here,* a freckling of the light,
as where parts curdle up

to fetch a whole – and the birds lift up –
and from the undulant swagger-stabs of peck and wingflap,
collisions and wobbly runs – out of the manyness –
a molting of the singular,
a frenzied search (upflapping, heavy) for cadence, and then
cadence found, a diagram appearing on the air, at arctic heights,

                                    an armoring
the light puts on – stagger of current-flap become unacrobatic industry,
                                        no tremble in it,
no echo – below, the freeway lustrous with accurate intention –
above us now, the sky lustrous with the skeleton of the dream of
                        reason – look up! –
Jacob dreamer – the winged volumetrics chiseling out a skull
for the dream –

So Sure of Nowhere Buying Times to Come

I .

I understood that there must have been.

And then the two folds of this world.

Towards us, thus marking time in time.

A gaping hole:

the *yes* suspended in the amniotic sac:

the end.

That there must have been.

That there might have been.

2 .

I understood then, in the intersection.
At the heart of the cross, in the traffic jam.
No matter that the light had changed.
The long mechanical howls going up from the gridlock.
As if a stairway had collapsed,
and we, each with our single destination at the core,
there inside the car –
(the point-awaiting-us now beating at the core),
(beating above the hum, mid-air, mid-car, yet wrapped by the ticking,
                                  honking shell) –
(by the shell of measurement, by the dream of passage) – as if we
were the rungs, the individual upwardgoing steps,

now crumbled in a heap
down here, having forgotten, each, the place we naturally once held,
there in that runged and buoyant upwardness . . .
Each with our right-measurement of hope,
the way an upwardness contains the dry backbone of hope,
construes it, like the rising of pitch in assertion,
or a gazelle fleeing up a slope,
constantly looking back, to see how far,
always a slight curve as we move towards purification.

3 .

A churchbell rang. A sawed-off lodgepole-limb stared out.
The traffic, bit by flaring bit, dressed by light, then by noonlight,
stayed there. Like a lid on a thing.
Like a gigantic bronchial growth devoid of breathing room.
Us watching the cross grow deeper, longer,
with all the glitziness of blessing,
the everyone-who-is-us constantly arriving, the four streets filling,
the four directions meeting, blurred,
in us,
the spot outside consequence, the blind, whorled spot,
where there is no longer push, or inch along, or halt,
and you should turn the motor off,
let the keys hang, the glittery tailfeathers of the bird
up to its eyes in ignition,
let it hang,
put the hands down into the strangely distant lap,
put the hands down, the eye in its anxious glancings down,
till the lid seems to release the Emergent altogether from its flow,
and lowers,
letting the circle of outwardness narrow,
the hurry, like a deep root stilling, abiding,
the stalk-end slimming,
the filmy thicknesses of to-and-fro narrowing,
the parts of the picture the glance sews up

beginning to break into separate puddles –
oh what aftermath of what great storm is this –
featurelessness settling its flyapart dust
on the one who predicts, on the one who follows,
on the yew bushes, on the republic,
on the traffic jam undeferrable,
in the homesick country. . . .

4 .

In that country, where the last thought sank to the floor, amid the
gleaming tailpipes and the newly laid-off, just above the stony chips of
specific destinations – held firm in flesh like bullets flesh survived – gently,
airily – where the thrumming batteries beggar motion – *what breaks down
breaks down* – in that unmaking, that stalling – eyes mid-height in their
windowframes – unable to catch other eyes for the gleam – there, in the
third minute of the noon hour, twitching slightly then rising on the
widening circles of accumulating exhaust, a small brown plastic grocery-
bag, empty, handle-straps pointing earthward, apricot-beige, soapsud
beige, like a voice in the next room one can't quite make out, rises, up
into the throat, the congestion, up high, in the grip of heat-fumes and the
nervous embroiderer's pause – hand mid-air, needle midflight – dream
tired but knowing still to rise – lifts beyond the picture – as if intended all
along – and the leaves whispering, at the crook of each curve the leaves
collecting – the eye, no longer singing in tune with the collecting brain,
watching the bag rise – spell with a name on its swollen belly – almost
sinking now above the rows – only to catch again on something clockwise,
updrafting, now gathering shine, now quarrying the emptiness for furling
laws and, up, up, wielding utter particularity in this pregnant bagfulness,
and so on . . .

The Guardian Angel of Self-Knowledge

How razor-clean was it supposed to become,
the zero at the core of each of these
mingling with leaves as they fork up in wind – bright yellow
                                                distillations of –
uprising evidence of this one world's gigantic
curvature – how clean, how denuded of *their* foliage,
these desperate, aimless ones in twos along the built-up paths,
in ones in corridors, these ones so skillfully grouped up
in liquid clutches of impermanence,
now taking the long way back along the lake,
now in the auditorium beaten upon by wind and then a little
rain. They look in their envelopes.
They look on their paper calendars, under their tongues,
stare at the shadows their bodies cast, stare at the shadows their
                                                folding-chairs cast,
with each glance something like a leaf let loose,
I watch it float, each eyelashed lurching forward, each hoarse
and giddy self-appraisal, I watch them
let it go, each owner standing so stilly now behind his words as they
                                                are given up,
on lunch-break, beside the phone-booth where one's crying
                                                softly now
into the glistening receiver, beside the bookseller, the fruitseller
where one comes right to the warm brink
of a yellow pear – oh from here
it looks so like a dream of shelter –
the way that reaching hand mimics the eye, romancing,
the way it quickens at its root, desiring,
the other one now rooting in a pocket for some change,
and other ones now touching a chin, a lip, an index-finger rough
on a cheek, as if to wipe away a glance – down there – oh how much
                                                must I see – how clean

did they want to become,
shedding each possibility with gusts of self-exposure,
bubbling-up into gesture their quaint notions of perfection,
then letting each thought, each resting-place, get swept away –
because that was *not what I meant* – *was not at all* –
and since the future isn't real, is just an alarmclock,
where the last domino can finally drop,
wearing a street-address around its medicated neck –
oh that – of course – the wound we cannot medicate –
you know – the room of icons so preserved we move them round to fit
the furniture, opinions nestling in them, down in the folds, the inlays,
opinions and calculations and bits of stardom
right down in there in the grain of the icons,
some truth in there too now, maybe in the form, who can tell,
maybe even some ecstasy, some little monstrosity,
though it doesn't matter,
since we can't tell the difference,
since it's all pre-recorded, or something like that –
who will they be when they get to the bottom of it,
when they've stripped away the retrospect, when they've peeled away the
orphanhood, the shimmering merriments of consolation?
How will they feel the erasures erase them?
Who will they resemble when they're done with resemblance?

Little Requiem

The reason confiscated. The reason nowhere to be
found. Blowing this very paper now
    out of my hands
if I would
    let it go –
The *reason-for* – something I'm waiting outside of, again today,
up at the fence, at the gate,
standing here very still –
And it is not gray, and it is not stone,
but small gray bushes – sage – with field of lupine all
around – the whimsical divine – no hint – behind it now the sun going
down – no hint – the beams tendentious, red –
at their lean-end laving the vast
    commemoration of
magenta which in these silent millions bends,
allowing wind-like bars of some insistent ditty
through. . . .
No hint of what this holds inside it though.
Flame-pink, rose, crimson and small ugly purple mix.
There is a speckling where some clouds won't let
sun through. There is a clattering where over-much
of lupine breed and pure sun makes them happen
more. It pushes and invests. It loads them down with
happening. No back-of-the-mind allowed. All
front, inherent, tinted-through with being till you
have to care. No hint of
what is locked in there, although I too am made to come

before it every day, and wait, and lean, and listen stilly for
some news.
Something *was* led away at dawn.
Something was locked away.
And yet what's here – what's left behind – is hardly
what was promised – hardly *there* – hardly
(not to reduce the thing) not there –
(and if the man was young they killed his father)
(and if the man was married they took his wife)
(unto the next squad)(unto the quiet and
deserted hills) (so we dig in) (so they
dig in) – the children crying, the light dramatically now
clattering on
across the once-again mint-condition end-of-day –
the swatch of sky issuing commemorative editions of . . .
If I wait closely where I look,
there are, in bips and blips,
small anthems being sung. They're in the
register where everything is choked into the forced
becoming visible – oh guards of the
imprisoned prisoner – no hint – no hint wherever my eye
scoops and rips – no hint in the pastels, in the shorn
fabulation of
space/time,
in the account field, light and color give – no hint what lisps
the windy promises of meaning in –
or what, withholding, under cover of form,
accepts, back-turned, breath-held,
the mild applause of miles of lupine,
the pleased crescendos where the eye joins lupine in
the borrowings of light –
bowing, accepting raucousness
where gaze and miles of weeds and seedpods
mix with wind – all of me now
standing on line, barely able to make out
what, there in the day, is held

against its will –
not wanting to go deeper-in, really, of course,
no matter how much I love,
not wanting to stay out here, in the reddish glow,
in the lower-right-hand corner, any
longer, either – unrecognized – a lazy river
glowing in the middle distance – no, no,
it has been led away, it is being led away,
a chill on its brow, somewhere a candle blowing-out (but by
    mistake),
and in the front room something
crying, something pretending not to notice as
it's led away, is being led away, the sky now
aqua, and beyond – oh, beyond – no color regions and then the
disappointing sequel – nighthawks,
certainties, denials, triumph over sorrow, triumph
    over pain.
The rest is darkness – no – the rest is optional.
Poking ahead, a little reasoning like insect-hum.
And then   no sound.
In the dark, cells dividing, cells
dividing further . . .
Something remembers them always and everywhere.
Always and *everywhere.* How consent to that   honor –

Willow in Spring Wind: A Showing

Pointless homesickness. Pointless shudderings.
Wind now clockwise: surrendering this way.
Wind now counter: surrendering that.
Wide tree with its good throat up from the dark
flinging forth embroiderings of inaudibles,
limbs jerked like a *cough* – then like a credo, flung –
then *broken oars,* then oars not broken at all but thrumming in
unison into
the open sea of my
watching.
Clasp me, trellis of glancings,
delicatest machine –
body of the absconding *god* –
replacing something (I know not what) –
undulating, muttering liquidly . . .
Is it my glance or is it the willow kneeling wildly now
as if looking for corpses,
dragging its alphabet of buds all along the gravelly walk –
scraping – ripping – along the seemingly insatiable
hardnesses of gravel? Also the limestone wall they slap. . . .
Where is the sharp edge that we seek? Where
the open mouth? –
the true roughness – halo distended –
glittering with exaggeration –
dazzling the still philosophies –

The Guardian Angel of the Private Life

All this was written on the next day's list.
On which the busyness unfurled its cursive roots,
pale but effective,
and the long stem of the necessary, the *sum of events,*
built-up its tiniest cathedral . . .
(Or is it the sum of what *takes place?*)
If I lean down, to whisper, to them,
down into their gravitational field, there where they head busily on
into the woods, laying the gifts out one by one, onto the path,
hoping to be *on the air,*
hoping to please the children –
(and some gifts overwrapped and some not wrapped at all) – if
I stir the wintered ground-leaves
up from the paths, nimbly, into a sheet of sun,
into an escape-route-width of sun, mildly gelatinous where wet, though
mostly crisp,
fluffing them up a bit, and up, as if to choke the singularity of sun
with this jubilation of manyness, all through and round these passers-by –
just leaves, nothing that can vaporize into a thought,
no, a burning-bush's worth of spidery, up-ratcheting, tender-cling leaves,
oh if – the list gripped hard by the left hand of one,
the busyness buried so deep into the puffed-up greenish mind of one,
the hurried mind hovering over its rankings,
the heart – there at the core of the drafting leaves – wet and warm at the
zero of
the bright mock-stairwaying-up of the posthumous leaves – the heart,
formulating its alleyways of discovery,
fussing about the *integrity of the whole,*
the heart trying to make time and place seem small,
sliding its slim tears into the deep wallet of each new event
on the list
then checking it off – oh the satisfaction – each check a small kiss,

an echo of the previous one, off off it goes the dry high-ceilinged
                                        obligation,
checked-off by the fingertips, by the small gust called *done* that swipes
the unfinishable's gold hem aside, revealing
what might have been, peeling away what should . . .
There are flowerpots at their feet.
There is fortune-telling in the air they breathe.
It filters in with its flashlight-beam, its holy-water-tinted air,
down into the open eyes, the lampblack open mouth.
Oh listen to these words I'm spitting out for you.
My distance from you makes them louder.
Are we *all* waiting for the phone to ring?
Who should it be? What fountain is expected to
thrash forth mysteries of morning joy? What quail-like giant tail of
promises, pleiades, psalters, plane-trees,
what parapets petalling-forth the invisible
into the *world of things,*
turning the list into its spatial form at last,
into its archival many-headed, many-legged colony. . . .
Oh look at you.
What is it you hold back? What piece of time is it the list
won't cover? You down there, in the theater of
operations – you, throat of the world – so diacritical –
(are we all waiting for the phone to ring?) –
(what will you say? are you home? are you expected soon?) –
oh wanderer back from break, all your attention focused
– as if the thinking were an oar, this ship the last of some
original fleet, the captains gone but some of us
who saw the plan drawn out
still here – who saw the thinking clot-up in the bodies of the greater men,
who saw them sit in silence while the voices in the other room
lit up with passion, itchings, dreams of landings,
while the solitary ones,
heads in their hands, so still,
the idea barely forming
at the base of that stillness,

the idea like a homesickness starting just to fold and pleat and knot

itself

out of the manyness – the plan – before it's thought,
before it's a *done deal* or the name-you're-known-by –
the men of x, the outcomes of y – before –
the mind still gripped hard by the hands
that would hold the skull even stiller if they could,
that nothing distract, that nothing but the possible be let

to filter through –

the possible and then the finely filamented hope, the filigree,
without the distractions of wonder – .
oh tiny golden spore just filtering in to touch the good idea,
which taking-form begins to twist,
coursing for bottom-footing, palpating for edge-hold, limit,
now finally about to
rise, about to go into the other room – and yet
not having done so yet, not yet – the
intake – before the credo, before the plan –
right at the homesickness – before this list you hold
in your exhausted hand. Oh put it down.

Untitled One

A curtain rose. I felt an obligation.
I tried to feel the thing that blossoms in me,
here in my seat, assigned,
the whole world intelligently lit
up there in front of me.
I tried to feel the untitled thing that blossoms in me.
The abnegation that doesn't stutter, not at all, not once.
Or no, that stutters once and once only.
What the days are a rehearsal for: *breathe in, breathe out.*
What the held breath is ventriloquial for,
the eyes quickly shut then scribbled
                          back open
again – rasping martyrdom –
the glance once again shouldering the broadcast out there, the loud
                          flat broadcast,
the glance ambushed once again by the apparent warmth of the picture.
I blinked. Tomorrow came. Nothing *came true.*
Birds scattered and the minutes clucked, single-file.
Daggering, talkative, the breaths ministered to nothingness.
A tight bond, theirs. An hysterical love. *Never mind* the things said –
those robberies. *I love you,* they said. Or *in a broader sense*
this example suggests . . . I tried to feel the days go on without me.
Walking in the park: a small tin of shoe-polish
nestled in the grass. From over the trees
the names of people were called out via loudspeaker.
Then there were numbers: the score, incessant coarse ribbon, floated by
                          elegantly,
then smeared itself all over the sky. . . .
The small hole inside I'm supposed to love:
I tried to house it – no, I tried to gorge it.
I hovered round it with sentences to magnify the drama.
I cloaked it with waiting. I whispered *don't be afraid*

and petitioned it with rapture – the plumed thing – the cross-dressed
lingering – dramatic – all my thin secrets giddy,
all my whispers free-spending . . . Tomorrow came.
Slowly it scattered. Then it came again – first fragile, eyes closed,
then, peeling away its cellophane, eyes striating open,
it did it again – and each time so easy; first blurring a bit, then, nearing 5,
the sparrows ascribble, the magnet rising, tomorrow
starting to strip itself clean again of itself. But casually. Tirelessly.
And without innuendo. Just oh so plucky.
Peeling the minutes off, the little white worms.
Quavering up to a strong fine whiteness.
High varnish. Yet noncommittal.
Giving thanks – or so it
seemed – then backing away, unexpurgated, sort of dis-
                      figured.
Then, again, tomorrow came. Never a chorus, only the hero.
And tomorrow, and tomorrow.
One after another, up into the floodlights.
I tried to feel the story grow, name by name,
one at a time. My eyes grew heavy, I could feel my attention slipping.
I tried to shoulder the whole necklace of accidents.
I waited for them all to reappear at the end.
To take a bow. All at once. All together. That I might remember.

Untitled Two

And shades approached. A masonry of shades, one in a
parking lot. Give him the darkest inch your mind
allows. Hide him in _____ if you will. But where?
And *fearless truth,* where is the thing?
And excellence, and skill, all throbbing in the parking lot.
And fashion, too, and brute strength, flickering. . . .
One that did earn an honest living. One like a statute
– lean – one like some gold someone is looking for,
one gray-eyed like a verdict, one ribbony with bits of valor,
or is it *stringy* now with *blips of laughter?*
The parking lot coagulates, quasi-maternal, and strict
with cradling unnumbered slots – one tall one fingering his hair
as he arrives, one coughing as he keeps on wondering.
They gather round, gloat, tangle, clot – they're many-eyed – they forage.
Over the gleaming fins and hoods, they seem to chatter.
The windshields singe with them, but then they clear.
Overhead sparrows snarl-up, and river, dive,
making a dark clean thought, a bright renown,
and quote each other endlessly,
and throng in hundreds in
surrounding trees.
The shades have liquefied.
I try to think them up again.
The banks of cars – the lot is filling up – now oscillate
in morning sun. And sunlight, toothless now,
how it keeps drinking in. And thinking, thinking.
Until the walled-up day hives-open once again.
And they foam-out along its veins. Syllable by syllable.
I give them liberty. They gnarl, they sweep over the hubs,
into the panes, they fill the seats.
Somewhere the tea is cold. Somewhere the fire is almost dead.
Somewhere a fear that has no form.

And someone thinking they are *home at last*.
The past is hanging from a beam.
Around us, toying, like a gigantic customary dream,
black water circles, perishing and perishing,
swirling black zero we wait in,
through which no god appears,
and yet through which nothing can disappear,
a maximum delay, a sense of blurred desire in it,
a slumbering, a catch-all mirror for the passers-by,
silky frontier in which it is all saved – the
voices of the girls now walking through, vaguely hysterical,
their plaids and lycra staticky,
the exemplary hair-bow twitching in the light,
crustaceous mylar day must nibble at, gum at,
gold arm-in-arm the girls now walking through the shades,
most of which now course into the long parked jewelry
of cars, so that they hive-up algebraic in their rows,
among the hundred worn, black steering wheels,
gigantic sum of zeros that won't add,
scoring the rippling field in which they wait,
gear-shifts and knobs and dials bearing the news,
fish-eyed rear-lights squinting alternative genetic codes,
and through us now, on break, the hurrying girls,
their voices swirling up – impregnable – frayed-edged – because one of
        them is earnest now, is lowering her tone,
and four of them begin enameling the light with deep
                                choked listening,
and then another takes her turn, voice rising quick and bright,
and two now interrupt – high-heeled – scales of belief,
quick blurtings-out like a bright red jug
raised high into the waves of light,
which their onrush of chatter fills now, spills,
and then a hard remark, slammed in, a lowering again
of tone, quick chitter from the group, low twist of tone
from in the midst, and then a silence – like a wing raised up,
but only one – a hum all round, heads facing forwards

in the cars, heads pointing forwards in the cars,
anti-freeze fingering daylight near some tailpipes, *here* and *here,*
a brutish click, sound of black-water lobbying,
and then one girl, like a stairway appearing in the exhausted light,
remembers the *reason* with a fast sharp gasp,
and laughter rises, bending, from the chalice of five memories,
as they move past us towards the railing of the lot,
one stepping over, quick, one leaping high, giggling – red hair above her

                                                     as she

drops – two whispering, one hands in pockets looking down
as she, most carefully, leans into the quick step
over the silver rail – oh bright forgetting place – then
skips to catch up with the rest,
and the rail gleams, and the rail overflows with corrugated light.

Flood

So in the cave of the winds he prisoned the north wind.

(no, it's too heavy, besides, how shall I put it)

And the north wind and the west wind and such others as

(sometimes the mood of a moment, sometimes an almond tree)

as cause the clouds of the sky to flee, and he turned loose

(oh empty cupboards, waiting for sleep, sleep)

turned the southerly loose and the southerly came

(we are far into the cave of seem, uneven rain, how

shall I put it) came out streaming, with drenched wings

dripping, and pitch black (how the Prince would laugh)

darkness veiling his terrible

(in those days and how his stories)

countenance, his beard

(but look out this window)(how solemn you are!)

heavy with rain, his locks a torrent, mists his chaplet,

and his wings (and you slept) and his linens and his other garments

running with rain . . . .

2 .

Now his wide hands squeeze together the wide low-hanging

clouds. Crash and rumble. Cloudbursts. Rainbow.

We are so happy in our way of life.

Thunder fills the apartment like news then is re-
                              placed –
(because it's true?)

and then the doorbell rang –

and then the rainbow's there, light drawing water from
                           the teeming mud
and sucking it up into the cloud again. Nothing

remains. (To say how pleased). Although a rumbling's

drawn across the sky. And tiny insuck where the cigarette
                          is lit.
And hums. And clicks. And lower tones. . . . Well that will do. So in
                         the end
                         something
remains? But what? The crops aren't spared. The farmer

prays. See him now in his dark kitchen at the
                     seeping
end of day – back bent at prayer – right there at the heart

of events – the hollow inside him

swinging, dusty, Yahweh's gamble, Jove's quick

rage, and a sudden breeze at the very end now of
                              this day
lifting the curtains, lifting the tiny beaded seam of sun
                              in them –
something that won't rub off if you should wish

to take it in your hands. (Oh take it in your hands). Then it is night.

3 .

Next day, blue skies. Below, blue mud with sky in it.

Above, blue sky with its mud hidden –

mud opening its seams, mud slackening the hard em-
                              bankments –
to silt – to chalk – as if the whole thing should be
                    sky – field walls

dissolved – hedgerows string-streams – roots splayed –

roots rotted off – white slush – and cellwalls, slush –

and the honeycombing masonry that separates and breeds, slush –

whole hillsides of thread-thin ash-white roots exposed,

all running downhill, gleaming, watery,

slipping their threaded, knotted

source, and the stems
    are set free,
and the leafy ex-
    tensions of rootline, the sun's
outermost meta-
    morphoses, light's outstretched
nailtip, light's beckonings, light's green
    in-chatters with sun

now glazed-down
    darkly, drawn down over the newly-exposed scree –
wilty, syrupy –

    – (as if the whole world must dissolve again) –

scummy, sleek – all the stubby quickenings of difference now

crushed back into one inky mottling, dank – the world
                        a sudden ripening
over rock and then, in the rush, the world –

4 ·

Oh let the river horses run wild as ever they would.

Their hooves: the rocks amid the deep roots loosening.

Their heavy breathing: the acceleration; rivulets
                    venting in sudden
loose spots – whitewaters, incurlings –

foam and tossing of manes over bedrock, tossing
           where the muscle of taproot snaps –

gleaming withers where rock-lichens are stripped off, where
                difference is sanded

off. . . .

And they obeyed, running.

And the earth opened for them.

And orchards are swept away, grain stores and cattle.

And men and houses, bridges, (temples), (shrines with

holy fires) –

5 .

An anchor drags the still-green meadow. A dog

barks, or is it a piece of cornice floating by. A feature. A
                              distinction . . . Do you wish
                              to pick it up?
A living cow floats among the floating carcasses.

Dogs come swimming with curious wonders.

(It is an honor)(this carrying what is being said)

Sun fingers down, weakening, to the city-park
                              below;
row-houses; fencing; schools turning abruptly, catching
                              the light –
the private life, what is the private life, what is it
                              that is *nobody's*
                              business
through this glassless display-case,

through this length of hallway holding corridors of water?

Bass dive through the woods.

A wolf swims frantic by the floating lamb.

A living deer and a doll – dress wide with floating –

are borne along – (good night, sweet ladies, good) –

and the wild pig finds all his strength useless –

and is there impatience now? there is no impatience –

and the deer cannot outspeed the current –

and the wind tries to billow the surface of water
but finds itself slowed to a thick ripple –

and birds fly low looking for someplace to land –
one tumbles, exhausted, into the current –

and the wings are turned again and again by waters –
frothings, suctions: they change shape
                              slightly
but do not vary . . .

Those are not hills, nor are they caves –
(the deep has buried the hills) –

Those are not depths nor are they walls –
(the deep has taken the downtown in) –

Those are not pearls nor are they eyes-
(like a bored salesgirl, current gnaws the banks) –
and all whom the water has spared will now
                              begin
to starve.

Spelled from the Shadows Aubade

Trying to whisper *life came back,* the light came back.
It harshed-up the edges of the window-shade, curling its rims,
the room still grainy, dimpling,
and shinglings of shadows, layerings.
But the borders of the latex shade, braced against morning, gleamed.
The programming on the other side leaked – deftly, splashily –
the acidly magnanimous harvest of the outside through –
high-pitched, fringed or winged,
framing insistent plenitudes.
Oh not as if evening had found me.
Or even the winter   rushing.
Get up, get up. You are to walk and talk again, and breathe, and move.
And breathe.
Any manner of *want,* any world will do – any tint of mind –
lift up the shade.
You are the underside, thinking.
With your *humility,* with your colloquial plague *(honor, desire),*
and formulas for grief and loss. . . . and shadows of other
things   unrelenting.
Get up. You must believe – prompt – with a snap of the wrist –
and the shade slap-up with its skillful and hardly querulous *whir* –
It held you, once, the other side,
in its gossipy arms,
it seemed to gaze with its taut wide-awakeness
straight into your furious machine,
it wasn't a shabby love – it held –
sentences poured from it in alleyways, sometimes in avenues,
the carpenters moved through them always needed,
joinings held,
cashiers added up the sum and it rose up from calculation
onto limpid sleek receipts – we paid – the eucalyptus shone –
the walkie-talkies heard each other clearly and the road got fixed,

it was a curious love, it didn't think —
each-other seemed a kind of waiting.
I know how simple all this sounds, in the light of
the ignorant sleep — so green — we now must labor in . . . And yes,
it is nice in here, in the blur,
in the year, and then the year, in the sleep where nothing's won,
or lost, the shade leaking its ancient storyline,
shadows of flags — or are they birds — flapping across it now and then,
or maybe banners where the strong go by,
or clouds, or shrivelings of place, late leaves just now torn free,
or calculations tossed by a profounder logic — green? — I couldn't
tell from here.
In the end must come merciless ignorance.
In the end must come time wasted utterly.
Across the shade now hands without arms — a picnic of bits — generations of
seeds — or are they wings — or instruments — a business deal, an alphabet?
What are we supposed to fear? Look, the frame of light before me
yawns, a glittery arctic yawn, effulgent, blazing,
slack, without fatigue,
a little wind in it now swelling the shade, off-white,
dropping the shade, lightflecks spit forth, bright bits of busyness
a yawn frets forth, frame tacking left a bit then back,
emptiness foaming up.
No hero here — so sleep. Predestination gossips. Trophies splatter
against the shade where they are won, then lost, outside.
And then the sound of rain. Maybe a woman and a man
                                    running a bit
then clinging to a tree.

Oblivion Aubade

What dimensions must the defeat acquire, the homecoming,
scrawling all over my skin, my sickly peering in,
for me to finally hear the laughter? I know it's there,
beneath the glittering exterior-latex, beneath the storyline and then the loss of
storyline – quick, bright derision –
oh these musicians make insidious tones –
clawing the singsong of their instruments . . .
How mocked the glance
dipping about in this dawn becomes,
the mockery right up against
my retina, the envy in me blushing up against
the possible, the taste of the laughter as it slaps
my face, what a flat mask, what a lacerated singularity peering out.
A small thing, really, the laughter, it could be anywhere, now that the wind
revives against the walls, doodling, as if enamored of the sophistries,

                                               the trembling
thin midwinter strands, and bumps, and ontological vomitings
against the wall – the Duttons' wall, the Franklins' wall . . .
I saw it highlight then forget each twig, it held some light in it,
or, no, it twisted back, peeled back, some light,
and then the light resumed its place,
each shadow spurred, sprung open, made to lacerate,
flavored by wind, toil, guise – is that a lyre? is that the engine
incorruptible? – shadows in which the thing is hid,
mocked suitors all as she unweaves.
I was stealthy, and timid, then felt the tonguing-up of blame.
I looked in all the places I had been.
I summoned up my wrong
and made a brittle climate for it
and it swelled – I turned – it seemed the caravans had just gone by –
the grass looked tall, the tips conceived their paraphrase of wind.
Outside the children sang and ran in circles to

a tinny tune. Outside
the shepherd fetched the wide and liquid herd back in. Outside
morning attends, its mask approaches and attends,
crows the musicians strike up black flames,
in clouds themselves churning along
from their impossible place of origin – oh impossible.
Something – not an idea – a tiny velocity.
How it sharpens the edges of the singular.
How loud the guests all round us have become,
day molting off,
no footprints anywhere,
every glance a skin, a rag thrown on the pile,
which raises in place of the world its gigantic debris,
the site of the I, the game of catch,
the dog at the end of the snarling chain.
What was his name? How can he tell if he is mine?

Which but for Vacancy

Again today the dream. But *of* what?
The dream like a long slim tunnel we lay ourselves down in –
the lilies in the dust, the face that seems to shine
in the linoleum – blue – the thing we would strip down to if –
the melting snow allowing, the faint falling-sound receding . . .
But the nature of the dream will not appear for us.
It lightens the air immeasurably
as if it were itself
a kind of dawn,
but only its form appears,
a stillness too elaborate
for minds like roots, minds that *are* roots, to comprehend –
(when what we wanted most, of course, was to believe, be loved) – oh
                                        comprehension,
such a small hissing sound it makes on this still air, that
            exhalation,
little path in its own right
the dream lays down.
Now light through shutters on the wall
is laying the spine of a serpent
down – bright vertebrate near-interlinking
bits – its sentence moving sideways, up –
while elsewhere now *again* and *again* move their own side-ways, up,
and yet elsewhere, again, the Lord God's forming something from the
            blue sea-slime
and forcing breath–of–life into its face
again.
A cracked pod calls.
The thing on my wall now, slow, grows little fangs, of gold,
where safety-latch and shutter enter into
shadow-play. And I can feel the tunneling rivery needs of the dream
            dissolving,

and I don't remember how I am supposed
to keep it, keep it . . .
Because you see the wind is sharpening itself on rocks.
The sun is rising up against the house.
The walls are yellowing with it.
Don't you hear the faint filling-sound it makes,
bringing its birds?
It looks gigantically down.
And the ribbony avenue of the possible dream frays, thins –
what gate, where is the gate? –
and the *waiting* which laid itself, also blue, down in that track,
hoping to be poured, hoping to be led out like a tongue,
the waiting which had ceased to writhe – at least grant me that –
the hoping which had made waiting its combustion –
although still *wanting* –
starts to dissolve as the pictures come on, the distances,
its dearest tension foaming up a bit then drying thinly off, like foam,
      in sun,
saturated quite so suddenly by the apparent strengths of the story,
appointments and well-drawn fields and, closer-up, a saucer-magnolia
where one bud, today, has just begun to rip
into view.

Thinking

I can't really remember now. The soundless foamed.
A crow hung like a cough to a wire above me. There was a chill.
It was a version of a crow, untitled as such, tightly feathered
in the chafing air. Rain was expected. All round him air
dilated, as if my steady glance on him, cindering at the glance-core where
it held him tightest, swelled and sucked,
while round that core, first a transition, granular – then remembrance of
thing being

seen – remembrance as it thins-out into matter, almost listless – then,
sorrow – if sorrow could be sterile – and the rest fraying off into all
the directions,

variegated amnesias – lawns, black panes, screens the daylight
thralls into in search of well-edged things. . . . If I squint, he glints.
The wire he's on wobbly and his grip not firm.
Lifting each forked clawgrip again and again.
Every bit of wind toying with his hive of black balance.
Every now and then a passing car underneath causing a quick rearrangement.
The phonelines from six houses, and the powerlines from three
grouped-up above me – some first-rung of sky – him not comfortable,
nature silted-in to this maximum habitat – *freedom* –
passers-by (woman, dog) vaguely relevant I'd guess though he doesn't
look down,

eyeing all round, disqualifying, disqualifying
all the bits within radius that hold no clue
to whatever is sought, urgent but without hurry,
me still by this hedge now, waiting for his black to blossom,
then wing-thrash where he falls at first against the powerline,
then updraft seized, gravity winnowed, the falling raggedly
reversed, depth suddenly pursued, its invisibility ridged – bless him –
until he is off, hinge by hinge, built of tiny wingtucks, filaments

of flapped-back wind, until the thing (along whose spine
his sentence of black talk, thrashing, wrinkling, dissipates – the history,
                                        the wiring,
shaking, with light –) is born.

Sea-Blue Aubade

Dawn – or is it sea-blue – fills the square.
Two in a room asleep with that window.
And dark thinning inside the view.
And human breathing.
And freedom in the room like a thin gray floating.
And doctrine.
And other kinds of shine rising off the edges of things –
as if the daylight were a doctor arriving,
each thing needing to be seen . . .
Soon the sunlight
will want to be changed.
Will want to be caught up in the weavings of freedom.
To be caught up in the wide net and made to have edges –
light coming in, so acidly, with the strength of wind or an ox . . .
Outside, slowly, the grapes seem fatter.
The cat moves its tail once in sleep.
The silence is largest wherever an eye falls.
Somebody's glance smokes through the blues until they start to
feel . . . ?
But it is all chalky.
All asleep, all unalive.
An icy thing, even in its fluency,
the tree, the stone heroically built up into a wall,
each stone in the mind of its mason, elsewhere, asleep,
the cat in the sleep of its owner, the purple light, muscular,
more days, more nights, more roads, shouts, flowers,
all making towards what pebbled shore,
each changing place with that which went before –
and forwards, forwards, how it all contends,
across the crookedness to be itself, to be at last, the crown,
the jeweled asterisk that stops that very moment still,

the place the parallels, the cruelties, *do,* for just a fraction

of a pebbled instant,

meet – (save that to die I leave my love alone) –

possibly rain oncoming – on the sidewalk down below

could it be steps, or is it just the clock? –

does it arrive and dissipate? –

no, it splatters like

thousands of thoughts,

replacing all the listening –

sea of ideas – so blue –

although you can hear something like cuts in the blue –

and one can feel how the boat feels –

all of the freedom swirling and slapping round the keel, the here,

foaming round, as feelings – and still the pitch of the dawn

grasping at transparence, as if something like an *hour* were

trying

to plash in, and make, and make . . . ? what would it *make?* –

and in the suddenly awakening one:

an upwards glance, one take – a main-mast starting up –

sails glimpsing about, quick rules and suppositions – coalescings –

and then the single sturdier open gaze cast up: a stare: a fear:

why is father lashed to it?

why is mother singing?

Miscellaneous Weights and Measures

What carries the universal law as meaning secreted within
itself.
What transforms the flaws into feeling.
Like coming home early and finding it was already there –
whatever it is you were expecting to expect you,
the perception of the world as something that flows
away from you in all
the directions – inhering, smoldering – yet spiraling outward with the
                                   intractable, inalienable
welding of matter to
desire. Until it is possible to say
the minutes add up, round and hard, and that the sum is
                    this concentrated force
that flaps against my already ransacked floor, my eye, my flapping
doorway-in. . . . Or, no, not flapping, not even mildly tethered to a blessed
randomness, no, just stuck ajar, as if waiting blindly for
uncreated substance – oh how madly in love we are with that slip of
                                   a thing –
ajar, so she can show up anytime,
never mind protocol,
never mind the late hour, or the posted hours, or the recording
instruments counting up hours, never mind the
hovering demolishments the built-in cam unveils, never mind.
It is the recipe we want, the blessed instruments.
It is the law in her dress of things we want let in.
It is the world made strange again
we want invited in.
Without memories, without distance. Just sunlight filtering nothing in.
Us down in the kitchen.
Below us the previous times.
In here with us an egg that breaks,

yolk held up in the pale daylit reverie of integrity, walls of occasion
                                                    holding,
the hand mid-air, not stalling but not progressing,
the whites having cleared the deliberateness of motion,
down now, gone into time, the yolk still afloat among those
whom death has spared,
the hand stemmed-out from one remembering a face,
a version of a face, like a crater in the forgotten,
the day and the upholding hand and the suddenly remembered face
stitched-up together here, fretted-up tight,
no witness, not even me, and, no, not you,
whatever you might feel your role to be,
here in the hard-core certainty rationing out this page,
your eye all over it – the egg, glossy and oversexed mid-air,
itself a swollen version of the day – ingredient . . .
No, it is the horror we can't conquer
pushing itself against the pane of dailiness
we want, the other sceneless thing,
the frightful repast,
where there is no subject –
the law – the dress with no body pushing it along,
nothing beneath, the rule of feathers
without the wing, or even the idea of wing,
one early afternoon in June,
making supper,
not looking to one side or the other,
fingers holding the egg again, look it is whole, it has
come back
from another place.
Don't forget.

The Guardian Angel of Not Feeling

As where a wind blows.
I can teach you that.
The form of despair we call "the world."
A theft, yes, but gossipy, full of fear.
In which the "I" is seen as merely a specimen,
incomplete as such, overendowed,
maneuvering to rid itself of biological
precipitates – hypotheses, humilities,
propensities. . . .
Do you wish to come with me?
You know how in a landscape you see distances?
We can blur that. We can dissolve it
altogether. You know the *previous age?*
How it lacks shape until it's cut away by
love? We gust that lingering, moody, raw affection
out, we peck and fret until it's
gone, the flimsy courage, the leaky luggage
in which you carry round
your drafty dreams – of form, of hinged
awarenesses, all interlocking-up – dream on –
the chain is rattling that you've cast,
yet it is made of air, of less, look, here
it mirrors, here it curves
in space, here it resembles – quick – for just a
nanosecond – *happiness* – incorruptible whole –
how soothing, so real, a ledge above the
waterfall – You know, in music,
how you hear – you strain to hear –
the isolation of the meager, the *you* alone,
an *interim* bristling with arguments, illusions –
they are lesions, they are spreading across a naked
skin, a rolling, planetary stretch of human skin,

not like the feeling of an unseen presence,
not like – oh wave demolishing,
we're waiting for the phone to ring,
we're busy – no? – we cling – the versions
of the desolation we clock-out in lists, in
miles – The wave, the wave appears
but then withdraws, it ruffles at its rim
as *whereabouts,* moonlight thrashes in its
curl, clatters as inventory in its curl,
the wave – wake up – the wave I'll give you
tiny bits of if you'll still –
Postpone the honeycombing day,
let the sandbar rise up beneath us here,
the bed will do,
the spattering of texture, shade – brocaded shirtsleeve on
the chair – the corridor of mysteries
you call your hair – the masonry of your
delays – pen, paper, ink – my friend,
look at the ink, dip fingers through its open neck,
bring hand to lip – there – do it again, again,
blazon the mouth, rub in, exaggerate –
the little halo forms, around the teeth,
the mirror on that wall shows you the thing,
furious, votive –
oh look, the tiny heart
mouthing and mouthing its crisp inaudible black zeros out.

Against Eloquence

Then there was the sense of a vectored landing – very fast.
We decided it was speed after all that could carry us.
We decided to decide. The drowse lifted. Something resembling
    air
glinted. Elsewhere a violin – alone – just done warming up,
the lovely sequencing beginning, stillness decomposing
where the notes rise up into it. And in the alcove two people in black
kissing a long time. And the frontier where the notes pulse, fringe,
    then fray
the very same stillness we place our outlines
in, the very same one we have to breathe, and flare our tiny
    nets of words
into (who's there?)(what do you hear?)(what hear?)(still
there?) – the very same – we listen in there –
the zero glistens – the comma holds –
flames behind where the siren goes off,
where someone is killed but only *by accident* so you are free to
    cross the street now –
I watch the lovers a long time –
they kiss as if trying to massacre difference –
the alcove around them swarms its complex mechanism made to
    resemble emptiness –
the shoppers go by; some vacuum hums;
something unseen, under-used, tarnishes; the daffodils
endowed by the widow *x* flourish – the lovers gnaw – the lovers
want to extinguish something –
something I know how to kill with a word, a single word –
the violin roils across the square –
they fracture emptiness to tiny masks – put each one on –
here's *smile* – here's *clenched* –
here's *fear* – here's *more* – emptiness doesn't take notice –
downpour of architectural void doesn't disturb –

moderation of accumulative time,

vague fabric tossed over the fire

as if to squelch it, ripples in the heat –

daffodils enter the decomposition known as yellow –

edges of the patio pulse –

violin notes float, wrinkling, unwrinkling – no –

they are not wrinkled – the message not delivered – nothing

at the address now – notes rinsing nothing –

nothing bleached by their acid –

nothing illumined by the ten thousand red tulips –

by the caustic justice of such gleaming beds

    deployed by a city

to force a plaza. . . .

April. . . .

Now the lovers are burying their arsenal.

Now with their stillness they navigate as usual.

Don't you know it's upstream? Don't you know you are supposed

    to look?

Right at the place their mouths mark, the place their mouths

    puncture –

What is the void once it is forced to cross through fire?

That Greater Than Which Nothing

Even the plenitude is tired of the magnanimous, disciplined,
                              beached eye in
its thrall. Even the accuracy
is tired – the assimilation tired –
of entering the mind.
The reader is tired.
I am so very tired.
Whom will this worry henceforth – radiant striation of hall-light on
                                        pillowcase –
who will receive it –
couch, table, half-open drawer, the granulated dark in it,
the cup, the three glasses – stupefying promises we are supposed to
                                        receive –
The glance? braiding and braiding the many promises of vision?
The glance, however exiled, wanting nonetheless only to come full term
                                        into the absolute
orphanhood? *Do you really want to die?*
Do you not maybe want to *sleep it off,* this time, again?
Nothing moves but the cloth as you breathe.
Don't look up at the four corners – the four conquering
                              corners –
for the shape of mercy. It swarms.
It composes gray-eyed walls on which the trapped light plays
                              like fumes off
kerosene – light, light everywhere, beckoning with its epic self-
                                        sameness –
all round you, roaming, rough in your shoulders, sparkling,
regrouping – grain by grain, no oases, no conversation –
asking each granulated breath your deep sleep
                              blossoms
to yield to it, to marry up –

and other dimensions – sandy, windy – exact – unincarnate –
                              tireless dimensions –
metamorphic yet unpliant –
now sparkling, sparkling – it's the light, you can't keep it out,
room 363,
its century of wide-eyed wing-work splashing
              hither and thither like graffiti
over the featurelessness – distending – distending the nature of
the erasure – merciless in its lightheartedness

in which the living is forgotten to be living –

The Strangers

The hand I placed on you, what if it
didn't exist, where it began, shaking, the declension of
your opening shirt, dusk postponed in each glazed and arctic
button, pale reddish shirt – what if it doesn't
exist – these fingers browsing the cotton surface, swimming in the steadfast
                                                    surface –
what if there's no place it can exist
this looking for a place to lie down in,
to make a tiny civilization –
here between the moss and long corridors of afternoon light –
between the exaggerations of the ornamental yews
laying themselves in day's slow caress across the brick apartment
                                                    house,
nothing voracious, nothing groping to make a plan find a place,
one of us against a tree now, one of us like a shadow
over water, one of us begging, one of us taking
                              measures,
thinking, rethinking,
between Wednesday and Thursday,
what if it doesn't exist, the place
where this hand lay flat for the first time
against your heart, cotton-denim and flesh
                              between,
to take it forever, first-fruit, from its limb,
tongue-tied, door slamming, cars stalled-out at traffic
                                        light –
is it a muscular place?
is it a cadence this open palm wants?
betrothed to the instant,
swearing allegiance,
a little dialogue between us like footprints,

is it the wingbeat itself it would cross through the
                              envelope of flesh
to get, this hand flat on you now, a badge, an x-ray,
homing in, an hypothesis, monosyllabic,
over the supple, gossipy, tin-can heart – unrelenting –
to make you exist –
Whose names does the wind riffle through, trying to see us?
And behind us: these tulips appearing out of nowhere –
the soil opening its thousands of lids. So easy.
A thumb at a time. Whole hands. Grappling back up.
They're flowers because they stop where they do.

Studies in Secrecy

The secret we don't know we're trying to find, the thing *un-*
seen,

is it ironic? is it a sign of anything? – raw
vertigo

the suction-point of which we now are trying to feed
our lives

into – the point devoid of ancestry, the bullioned point,
so sleek,

dwindling yet increasingly aswarm,

the chittering of manyness in it as it is made to
clot

into a thrumming singleness – the secret – the place where the words
twist –

we are looking for it everywhere –

we look on my breast, we try the nipple,

we look in the gaiety of your fingertips, the curriculum
of caresses

twisting and windy in the architecture of
my neck, my

open mouth – we look in your mouth –

we look, quick, into the-day-before-yesterday – we look
away –

we look again into your violent mouth,

into the edifice of your whisper, into the dwindling oxygen
we eat,

inhaling, exhaling –

we look into the glassy eyes we have between us –

we try not to shift, we stare,

there seems to be an enclosure in there, maybe a struck
note, an hypothesis,

we look in each other's hair

as in ripe shrubs bearing and withering,
we feel time glide through the room, between our legs,
round through our glance – we think we can look in the walled-up
                                                  thoughts –
we let our nights get tangled, we try to stare –
if something happens – the phone rings, a cigarette is lit,
maybe a massacre, maybe in spring the curtain
blossoms – gossamer – we look in there –
then we go back to the green-eyed heat, and stare,
beating on the icy film between each thing, knocking, tapping,
                              to see what's happening,
"the wasteland grows; woe to him hiding wastelands
                    within"(*The Portable*
Nietzsche –Viking '54 – we look in there),
also look in "Alas, the time is coming when
man will no longer shoot the arrow of his longing
beyond man" – "the string of his bow has forgotten
to whir" – it is a haze – the radio's
              on, the automated
churchbells ring – we start the matter up again, we cry, we finger
the folds – we open our lips – we bite our necks –
don't make me explain, one wing of it is soot, one wing
                              of it is blood,
we lick it, we nibble aimlessly, not so much tired as
increasingly ignorant – the minutes barbed now – the
blue streak where we hear a siren louder now,
our shoulders glistening, our backs greasy with hope,
foraging now (we try the book again) (we try putting things
                              in each other
to see how much room)("the earth has become smaller
                    and on it hop
the last men") so that we have to start
saying the words again (the last men live longest) –
I love you I say – poor secret, did you need us?
did you need us to find you? –

(live longest — *we have invented happiness,* they say) —
I love you, you say, rising among the motes, the spores —
and *forever and forever* like a sleeve we slide the hissing secret in —
the golden-headed, the upthrown — have invented *happiness* say the
    last men —
and blink.

The End of Progress Aubade

(EURYDICE TO ORPHEUS)

Sleep. Sink. Don't let the ceiling in.
The squad-car gliding watery around the block.
The day starting to float-in through the louvered cracks.
Glasslike, embellishing.
Forget the making now –
float in the repetitions of the far –
shift and unfasten in
the swarming lessenings –
your face downturned – the roomdarks floating towards
the lure of – the limits of –
your barely breathing
pallor – sleep –
lie with the whisperings in which you are
      still free –
lie tightly intertwined – unopen – petal yourself round
        the stamen of
some green unuttered syllable –
Oh look at you –
as music slumbering over her instrument,
I bend so close your breathing warms the violent
       idleness
of my sealed lips – I would not have
the daylight touch you –
I would not have the magnifications, the integrations
touch you – the thoughts – the faith that *inly*
feels – (they filter in: edges tongue up into the visible) –
nor would I (as music) (slumbering) ever touch you
and risk awakening the song again –
my mouth at your still fingers now (though not so much

as grazing them) – shut lids leaned close to where the breaths
                                   you leak
can moisten them.
I am meticulous.
The gods are gone.
I take your breath into my hair – nothing so clean
as this my microscopic distance from you – a clean so very small
even the sixteenth-note, the insect-wing, would snag – and yet
for all the tinfoiled bits of light
starting to streak your pillowed
                   sleepblank
brow – pooling like halogen into your open fist –
for all the ceiling's leaning in – for all my face, my open
                         gaze landing on you –
my thought, my sequencing and chording brain –
and the tonguing down of the airy fire
demanding now we rise and witness it, play it,
all taut-strung crevices, serrations, frets –
("composed at Clevedon, Somersetshire") –
for all, I would not touch you, even so lightly, Sir, again,
now that the siren's going off, elsewhere, somewhere,
darkening, refolding the surrounding air,
to make you stay there now,
to keep your thought sunk down, weighed down
the steep incline – flung down –
to where there are
no gales, no wings,
no world so filled, no life within –
turned over and over and over and over
                   by hands
not mine
whose silky-black examination
finally is free
of love –

Red Umbrella Aubade

On my way home I hear, somewhere near dawn,
forged and stamped onto the high air,
                    one bloodshot
cardinal-call – bejangled clarity gripping firm –
casting its pulverized acrylic in-
                    terrogation
out – plain out –
first once like a dropped red stitch
and then again like the start of
            a silky argument
unfolding. . . .
Shadowy as gloaming will allow,
I stand beneath. The paraphernalia of my listening
stands beneath.
At every periphery, the glinting –
like a chafing of the visible by the roughnesses of night
till the raw, the swollen, the bristling edges of things
are ground-down-to again – the glinting
almost begins – yet how I want to make it
last, sightless narration,
            untilled,
before the cacophony of edges – forking, collating –
ignites again, orchestral . . .
For you – for us – I know I should listen hard,
but to penetrate what? –
my knowing to listen itself an aftermath of red,
my wanting to stop *for you*
already a cough
from my concealment
cracking the granular
solitude. . . .
Where are we going, friend?

I'm in the incarnate, hurrying home.
Where is the gladness – the oasis – the unyielding gleaming
                                        opacity
you can't see through – reflecting, reflecting – ?
The winglike silences of just-before-dawn slur on.
Tiredness blossoms like a path, vectoring me.
Then, sugary at first, then monstrous, cuneiform,
as if a microscopic chain had rattled once –
bony lightning – invisible inscription –
the call is returned – or, no, another call, almost identical,
is cast – like a hoofmark on the upper registers –
across the housetops – as far as the park? –
and then the first again, at its stronghold up to the left of me,
and then the answering call again, the back-and-forth syringed, perfectly
designate, abyss all round the arc – above, below –
and the arc not suffering time – unwrinkling everything –
no dialogue,
no errancy,
just the red currency of back and forth,
me in the wide romance of aftermath,
a muscle clenched between them – call and call –
like a bullet's path yet where nothing is crossed,
no garmenture ripped, no body entered –

and then an aftertaste, as of ashes, in my mouth,
from listening –

The Hurrying-Home Aubade

A gust inside the god.
A listening sliced deep into the hearable.
A little temple of bone and sinew built,
blood rushing round.
A pasturing of molecules and thought . . .
Dawn's weaving murmurings all round my head.
So carefully. Arranging it.
Not yet do the silky windows which,
all round me, still buried in last night's acid
      cornerlessness,
underneathly glow — not yet do they
appear and stare — the folds of space
      still hold them tight —
unuttered yet full ready in the throat —
so many windowpanes — I feel them everywhere,
their mother-of-pearl-edged stupefied midwifery
about to start to glow again — (bright star!) —
cornered and comprehensive, row by row,
and then the offices of *love,*
assembly-line of little kisses down the block,
the sifting of the framed, the seen, from the mad flanking fires of . . . —
(are you all right? was it a dream?) —
the dawn like something rusty starting its engines up again —
the gears of thirst and gravity,
the numberless lids spanking awake,
and though I can't make out its frame,
a gate is swung, galactic gate, I hear the hinge,
the slavery raising itself chain by chain,
edges like little knives flooding the emptiness,
outlines radiating, innermost crevices rising up to be
      seen,
retrospect settling in, invisibly like dust,

self-containedness silting – here step, here lip –
here the forked ranking limbs, the skeletal sky
     between them
christening, incarnadine – and the slump of blossoming –
and crispness settling into the vaguer bloom, mottled by such
     grainy differencing
as light allows
before the sun begins to sift
     and card –
"they had almost reached the rim of the upper
     world" I think
"when afraid that she might slip, impatient
to see her bright beloved face" – some flowers appearing now
     and they,
from pressures I had not discerned before,
of light, of dew, bend heavy-headed, here and there,
     heads grazing loam – a little wind –
" the wound still fresh upon her skin"
(somewhere in here the bright beloved face)
until the boundary-lines begin to silver into place,
and the dogs of perspective gather round me,
and the dogs divide me up amongst themselves, the dogs of
     the given
– (her hands thin air)(the wound still fresh) –
and the doorways come clear, and the driveways,
and the hurry now
newly multi-faceted,
throats opening everywhere, squalls of place like insect-clouds
     coalescing,
my glances darting now, notional – my glances
tender-minded, yes, but prismatic,
the nationstate of my premises, the nationstate of my poised
     promises,
the little lashed metronome of the singular, helpless blink –
and how even lurching, squinting, refusing to mend, it
     mends, it

patterns – advantage helplessly taken by
    the taking
in – and the boundary-lines have
fallen – ("and under their tongues are mischief") –
and the dogs of difference are all around me –
and "I" am poured out like water.

Le Manteau de Pascal

I have put on my great coat it is cold.

It is an outer garment.

Coarse, woolen.

Of unknown origin.

❧

It has a fine inner lining but it is
as an exterior that you see it – a grace.

❧

I have a coat I am wearing. It is a fine admixture.
The woman who threw the threads in the two directions, headlong,
has made, skillfully, something dark-true,
as the evening calls the birds up into
the branches of the shaven hedgerows,
to twitter bodily
a makeshift coat – the boxelder cut back stringently by the owner
that more might grow next year, and thicker, you know –
the birds tucked gestures on the inner branches –
and space in the heart,
not shade-giving, not
chronological . . . Oh transformer, logic, where are you here in this fold,
my name being called out now but back, behind,
in the upper world. . . .

❧

I have a coat I am wearing I was told to wear it.
Someone knelt down each morning to button it up.
I looked at their face, down low, near me.
What is *longing?* what is a *star?*
Watched each button a peapod getting tucked back in.
Watched harm with its planeloads folded up in the sleeves.
Watched grappling hooks trawl through the late-night waters.
Watched bands of stations scan unable to ascertain.
There are fingers, friend, that never grow sluggish.
They crawl up the coat and don't miss an eyehole.
Glinting in kitchenlight.
Supervised by the traffic god.
Hissed at by grassblades that wire-up, outside,
their stirring rhetoric – this is your land, this is my *my* –

෫

You do understand, don't you, by looking?
The coat, which is itself a ramification, a city,
floats vulnerably above another city, ours,
the *city on the hill* (only with hill gone),
floats in illustration
of what was once believed, and thus was visible –
(all things believed are visible) –
floats a Jacob's ladder with hovering empty arms, an open throat,
a place where a heart may beat if it wishes,
pockets that hang awaiting the sandy whirr of a small secret,
folds where the legs could be, with their kneeling mechanism,
the floating fatigue of an after-dinner herald,
not guilty of any treason towards life except fatigue,
a skillfully-cut coat, without chronology,
filled with the sensation of being suddenly completed –
as then it is, abruptly, the last stitch laid in, the knot bit off –
hung there in Gravity, as if its innermost desire,
numberless the awaitings flickering around it,

the other created things also floating but not of the same order, no,
not like this form, built so perfectly to mantle the body,
the neck like a vase awaiting its cut flower,
a skirting barely visible where the tucks indicate
the mild loss of bearing in the small of the back,
the grammar, so strict, of the two exact shoulders –
and the law of the shouldering –
and the chill allowed to skitter-up through,
and those crucial spots where the fit cannot be perfect –
oh skirted loosening aswarm with lessenings,
with the mild pallors of unaccomplishment,
flaps night-air collects in,
folds . . . But the night does not annul its belief in,
the night preserves its love for, this one narrowing of infinity,
that floats up into the royal starpocked blue its ripped, distracted
                                        supervisor –
this coat awaiting recollection,
this coat awaiting the fleeting moment, the true moment, the hill, the
                                        vision of the hill,
and then the moment when the prize is lost, and the erotic tinglings
                                        of the dream of reason
are left to linger mildly in the weave of the fabric,
the wool gabardine mix, with its grammatical weave,
never never destined to lose its elasticity,
its openness to abandonment,
its willingness to be disturbed.

                                        ❧

July 11 . . . Oaks: the organization of this tree is difficult. Speaking
generally no doubt the determining planes are concentric, a system of
brief contiguous and continuous tangents, whereas those of the cedar
wd. roughly be called horizontals and those of the beech radiating but
modified by droop and by a screw-set towards jutting points. But beyond
this since the normal growth of the boughs is radiating there is a system of
spoke-wise clubs of green – sleeve-pieces. And since the end shoots curl

and carry young scanty leaf-stars these clubs are tapered, and I have seen
also pieces in profile with chiselled outlines, the blocks thus made
detached and lessening towards the end. However the knot-star is the chief
thing: it is whorled, worked round, and this is what keeps up the illusion
of the tree. Oaks differ much, and much turns on the broadness of the
leaves, the narrower giving the crisped and starry and catherine-wheel
forms, the broader the flat-pieced mailed or chard-covered ones, in wh. it
is possible to see composition in dips, etc. But I shall study them further.
It was this night I believe but possibly the next that I saw clearly the
impossibility of staying in the Church of England.

☙

How many coats do you think it will take?

The coat was a great-coat.

The Emperor's coat was.

How many coats do you think it will take?

The undercoat is dry. What we now want is?

The sky can analyze the coat because of the rips in it.

The sky shivers through the coat because of the rips in it.

The rips in the sky ripen through the rips in the coat.

There is no quarrel.

☙

I take off my coat and carry it.

☙

There is no emergency.

❧

I only made that up.

❧

Behind everything the sound of something dripping

The sound of something: I will vanish, others will come here, what is that?

The canvas flapping in the wind like the first notes of our absence

An origin is not an action though it occurs at the very start

Desire goes travelling into the total dark of another's soul
looking for where it breaks off

I was a hard thing to undo

❧

The life of a customer

What came on the paper plate

overheard nearby

an impermanence   of structure

watching the lip-reading

had loved but couldn't now recognize

❧

What are the objects, then, that man should consider most important?

What sort of a question is that he asks them.

The eye only discovers the visible slowly.

It floats before us asking to be worn,

offering "we must think about objects at the very moment
when all their meaning is abandoning them"

and "the title provides a protection from significance"

and "we are responsible for the universe."

৵

I have put on my doubting, my wager, it is cold.
It is an outer garment, or, conversely, a natural covering,
so coarse and woolen, also of unknown origin,
a barely apprehensible dilution of evening into
an outer garment, or, conversely, a natural covering,
to twitter bodily a makeshift coat,
that more might grow next year, and thicker, you know,
not shade-giving, not chronological,
my name being called out now but from out back, behind,
an outer garment, so coarse and woolen,
also of unknown origin, not shade-giving, not chronological,
each harm with its planeloads folded up in the sleeves,
you do understand, don't you, by looking?
the Jacob's ladder with its floating arms its open throat,
that more might grow next year, and thicker, you know,
filled with the sensation of being suddenly completed,
the other created things also floating but not of the same order,
not shade-giving, not chronological,

you do understand, don't you, by looking?
a neck like a vase awaiting its cut flower,
filled with the sensation of being suddenly completed,
the moment the prize is lost, the erotic tingling,
the wool-gabardine mix, its grammatical weave
– you do understand, don't you, by looking? –
never never destined to lose its elasticity,
it was this night I believe but possibly the next
I saw clearly the impossibility of staying
filled with the sensation of being suddenly completed,
also of unknown origin, not shade-giving, not chronological
since the normal growth of boughs is radiating
a system of spoke-wise clubs of green – sleeve pieces –
never never destined to lose its elasticity
my name being called out now but back, behind,
hissing how many coats do you think it will take
"or try with eyesight to divide" (there is no quarrel)
behind everything the sound of something dripping
a system of spoke-wise clubs of green – sleeve-pieces –
filled with the sensation of suddenly being completed
the wool gabardine mix, the grammatical weave,
the never-never-to-lose-its-elasticity: my name
flapping in the wind like the first note of my absence
hissing how many coats do you think it will take
are you a test case is it an emergency
flapping in the wind the first note of something
overheard nearby an impermanence of structure
watching the lip-reading, there is no quarrel,
I will vanish, others will come here, what is that,
never never to lose the sensation of suddenly being
completed in the wind – the first note of our quarrel –
it was this night I believe or possibly the next
filled with the sensation of being suddenly completed,
I will vanish, others will come here, what is that now
floating in the air before us with stars a test case
that I saw clearly the impossibility of staying

Manteau

In the fairy tale the sky
    makes of itself a coat
because it needs you
    to put it
on. How can it do this?
    It collects its motes. It condenses its sound-
track, all the pyrrhic escapes, the pilgrimages
    still unconsummated,
the turreted *thoughts of sky* it slightly liquefies
    and droops, the hum of the yellowest day alive,

office-holders in their books, their corridors,
    resplendent memories of royal rooms now filtered up – by smoke, by
must – it tangles up into a weave,
    tied up with votive offerings – laws, electricity –
what the speakers let loose from their tiny eternity,
    what the empty streets held up as offering
when only a bit of wind
    litigated in the sycamores,

oh and the flapping drafts unfinished thoughts
    raked out of air,
and the leaves clawing their way after deep sleep set in,
    and all *formations* – assonant, muscular,
chatty hurries of swarm (peoples, debris before the storm) –
    things that grew loud when the street grew empty,
and breaths that let themselves be breathed
    to freight a human argument,
and sidelong glances in the midst of things, and voice – *yellowest*
    day alive – as it took place
above the telegram,

above the hand cleaving the open air to cut its thought,
hand flung

    towards open doorways into houses where
den-couch and silver tray
    itch with inaction – what is there left now
to believe – the coat? – it tangles up a good tight weave,
    windy yet sturdy,
a coat for the ages –
    one layer a movie of bluest blue,
one layer the war-room mappers and their friends
    in trenches

also blue,
    one layer market-closings and one
hydrangeas turning blue
    just as I say so,
and so on,
    so that it flows in the sky to the letter,
you still sitting in the den below
    not knowing perhaps that now is as the fairy tale
exactly (as in the movie) *foretold,*
    had one been on the right channel,
(although you can feel it alongside, in the house, in the food,
    the umbrellas, the bicycles),
(even the leg muscles of this one grown quite remarkable),

    the fairy tale beginning to hover above – onscreen fangs, at the desk
one of the older ones paying bills –
    the coat in the sky above the house not unlike celestial fabric,
a snap of wind and plot to it,
    are we waiting for the *kinds* to go to sleep?
when is it time to go outside and look?
    I would like to place myself in the position
of the one suddenly looking up

to where the coat descends and presents itself,
not like the red shoes in the other story,
    red from all we had stepped in,
no, this the coat all warm curves and grassy specificities,
    intellectuals also there, but still indoors,
standing up smokily to mastermind,
    theory emerging like a flowery hat ,
there, above the head,
    descending,

while outside, outside, this coat –
    which I desire, which I, in the tale,
desire – as it touches the dream of reason,
    which I carry inevitably in my shoulders, my very carriage, forgive me,
begins to shred like this, as you see it do, now,
    as if I were too much in focus making the film shred,
it growing very hot (as in giving birth) though really
    it being just evening, the movie back on the reel,
the sky one step further down into the world but only one step,
    me trying to pull it down, onto this frame,
for which it seems so fitting,
    for which the whole apparatus of attention had seemed to prepare us,
and then the shredding beginning
    which sounds at first like the lovely hum
where sun fills the day to its fringe of stillness
    but then continues, too far, too hard,

and we have to open our hands again and let it go, let it rise up
                               above us,
    incomprehensible,
clicker still in my right hand,
    the teller of the story and the shy bride,
to whom he was showing us off a little perhaps,
    leaning back into their gossamer ripeness,
him touching her storm, the petticoat,

the shredded coat left mid-air, just above us,
the coat in which the teller's plot
    entered this atmosphere, this rosy sphere of hope and lack,

this windiness of middle evening,
    so green, oh what difference could it have made
had the teller needed to persuade her
    further – so green
this torn hem in the first miles – or is it inches? – of our night,
    so full of hollowness, so wild with rhetoric. . . .

The Shadow of Peter

Listen closely. These are not letters. They float,
slight shine perhaps – there where they mean –
and you can pronounce the *d,* friend, and the luscious *s,*
although none of it is really even in your mouth, is it,
more like a knock you're not quite sure you heard,
then someone opening the door, and a glance sliding in, rippling its
channel of desire
over to you. *Are you there?*
What is it the glance carries in its golden body when it reaches you?
What would it sliver open? – what smother?
The door like a stage-door, there to the side,
a dressing-room door, company not expected . . .
Yet here he is, the one-who-knocked,
wanting so to be seen – to be knitted up, chainmail of vocables – link
                                                            by link –
till even the air all round you suddenly seems to
shine – really now – there where it *means,*
or means to mean, because mostly of course it is
just talk, light tappings at the door and then the face of someone –
not looking for you at all, not at all – glancing *in* at you and then
      quickly away –
it must be further down the hall, you hear them say,
where the lock pronounces its name
and you see suddenly the pane, the window, rainbits on it,
splatters of grime – then shrieks down the hall
where the seeking-one is recognized
and the love is pronounced.
You imagine the glances meeting and the faces being seen.
You imagine the sensation of *recognition.*
The dear features grouped-up in their signature frame –

a thing seized-up into a form,
as if the glance were hung with images
of who one had always only been – *Oh I see you!*, the mother squeals
where the infant squints to see past
what's come to hide those crucial features now – the fluttery white hand,
flapping its too-thick wing to show a bit of lip –
nostrils and the glinting bit of eye
like the light at the end of some tunnel of course
except to the crawling one, looking up,
to see where the face has gone – to see it come flashing back –
suddenly whole – why? how? – then, in an updraft of decibels, vocables,
hushings and whisperings and small quick clues –
oh incomprehensibles – those syllables! – gone again –
behind the winged face –
oh but where have *we* gone, here? –
and the one who has come into the room wanted, expected,
suddenly opened to recognition,
who is he when he is taken-in by the acid refinement,
the filter, the prison of the realizing glance –
it's you, it's just you, exactly you, I see you – like a headlight between us
my glance sees you, takes you up, takes you in –
you are what I recall of your being you –
and me, do you see me, is the entanglement complete,
the furrow drawn out here between us,
and in it, fine seed, the act of recognition laid in . . .

2 .

Ascospore, Basidiospore, Carpospore – *(a minute uni-*
cellular reproductive or resistant resting body) –
Chlamydospore, Conidium, Endospore, Exospore –
(often adapted to survive unfavorable environmental conditions to
produce) – Megaspore, Microspore, Oospore, Telio-
spore – *(a new vegetative individual)* – Zoospore, Zygospore –
(morphologically a mass of protoplasm) – Compare *seed,*
statoblast, gemmule – a multilocular body,

which becomes free, that is difficult to destroy, a specialized
structure, a body or chain, a coat or layer – as in various smuts and rusts –
propagation by both budding and repetition –
a cyst, a cushion, a host, a tuft –
minute tubes in the wall –
erumpent crowded clusters of –
consistently typically of –
remaining permanently attached to –
absorbed by – distinguished from –
of flowerless plants – sporadic –
and they all went home – and at daybreak they brought a woman along
whom they had caught committing adultery –
and they said unto Jesus (making her stand there in full
view) Master,
this woman was taken
in the very act –
and Jesus stooped down –
and Moses in the Law commanded us
to condemn this woman to death by stoning,
what sayest thou? –
but Jesus stooped down –
they asked him this as a test –
that they might accuse him –
but Jesus bent over and wrote on the ground
with his finger –
and as they persisted in their questioning, he looked up
    at them –
then he looked down and wrote on the dirt
again.

Come now, let us go.

The Guardian Angel of Point-of-View

A mourning dove. And again what you suffer
seems, ah, as if yet unlived-through.
The bird keeps calling. You are in the middle
of the call.
There is thirsting in this work.
I must uphold – faultless – each outline – up –
each sloughing-off of meaning
into form. Ah. . . . The bird keeps calling.
Behold – says my headless swording-in – *this*.
A gibbering, then a surprising fastness, then the opulence of
the stilled thing, seen.
There is a thirsting for ever greater
                         aperture,
for ever more refined
beginning. Desire for a stillness that truly un-
folds. Thirst,
because I'm never wholly *in* creation,
unlike these I am compelled to witness, there, everywhere –
                         (any skull will do) –
seizing all too easily all that I split apart,
emptiness's vast ripe fruit.
Oh to taste the limits of the single aperture.
To have that one beam burn from one's head –
the snapping of a retina – no errancy –
and starched, voracious – (plunder without narration) –
this view the very drink for whom these drinkers are
created, these distances
uniquely meant to thread their narrow hurt –
the browsing mind encountering the filament of point-of-view,
the mind outstretched – at first so clean of greed –
a look you would call innocence for its
meandering delicacy,

a corridor of premonitions, footnotes, convoys of
intuitions all whispering at once
but slight – gravely steadfast though underneathly glutinous –
still moonlit, though now dawn refines, embroiders, im-
prisons . . . The bird has almost done.
And again what you suffer seems, ah, as yet
unlived-through – infinite detail the retina receives,
                                        thrashes,
transacts, parades. . . . Here's the corridor, the blade of
having seized the seen – how it narrows, how unlike the call it is now at
its very end. . . . What would you say these three low notes *lead to* – you,
                                                    eyelashed,
hunched forward just a bit in spirit,
your eye loudly sussurating down the suddenly wide open
                                        corridor,
licking the long walls awake,
cause and effect shuddering all down it as the running
                prosecution of the glance
forks past – oh pallors of the barely-seen –
bird still administering the yet-again overlooked
                                antidote –
angry radiance starting now to lurk
behind the blinds,
widow night-fragrances shivering-away weeping,
starving emptiness at the core of the long corridor
                coming awake – individuating –
first blood-shot down its inner lengths,
then flat, clean, quick, gusting with the suctions of
                                the possible –
oh anything – let them wake up, therefore,
discalced, refined – meandering supplicants
seeking a tyrant or a tyranny that won't reveal itself,
nearly-shy first-glancings a little advance cavalcade,
then coalescing, sensing the something that is
                missing here – beside? inside? –
beings so full of second-thought,

overwakeful, blurry with anticipation and hurry
and the sense, always, of *something being stolen* –
then the strewn, loose gems of tossed-out glances,
unstrung at first, blossoms in dry first-sunshine wind,
$\qquad$ scattering, against the wall. . . .
Why is it these branchings – these shadows of looking – grow manic with
seeing-through and seeing-through? $\qquad$
The stingingly empty light rising now
$\qquad$ out of the neveryet
through such nothings as these tiny blips of sight
$\qquad$ (or is it thought)
into the nevermore. . . . The cooing rises once, throaty up-pitch,
then thrice returns to one unchanging note – tiny blue steps –
no rising question marveling-up –
no drive-to-supposition tailoring down – no – three notes unvarying,
carrying a weight, a heavy little truth, there
on air's stalwart unpronounceable flat back –
$\qquad$ no flourishings
off which the suction-draftings of
the truth and its elsewhereness
spring – no – listen – three stressings of
no forwardness – selfsame – again selfsame – the path without the crumbs. . . .

The Guardian Angel of the Swarm

∝

inclension of   (endogenous)

crannies of   (exogenous)

labyrinth   swarm

teeming   unearthed   invagination   oscillation

collision   suppression

intubation   prefiguration

matter is marbled, of two different styles.

∝

It is the upper floor it has no windows.
It is a dark room decorated only
by a stretched canvas, diversified by folds,
as if it were a living dermis. Placed there, on the opaque canvas,
folds, cords, springs represent
an innate form of what we call knowledge.
But when solicited by matter
they move into action, trigger

vibrations, oscillations – a correspondence, even a communication –
between the two labyrinths,
between the pleats of matter and the pleats of the soul –

(matter is marbled, of two different styles) –

∝

But the universe appears compressed by an active force
that endows matter with a curvilinear or spinning movement,
following an arc that ultimately has no tangent.
And the infinite division of matter causes compressive force
to return all portions of matter to the surrounding areas,

to the neighboring parts that bathe and penetrate the given body –

Dividing endlessly, the parts of matter form
little vortices in a maelstrom, and in these
are found even more vortices, even smaller,
and even more are spinning in the concave
intervals of the whirls that touch one another –

an infinitely porous, spongy or cavernous texture without emptiness –

❧

unfolding is thus not the contrary of folding,
but follows the fold up to the following fold –
particles turned into folds that contrary
effort changes over and again –

❧

and every fold originates from a fold, *plica*
ex plica. . . . – an entre-deux, something
"between" in the sense that a difference is being
differentiated –

❧

and it is thus the world must be placed *in* the subject –
in order that the subject *be* for the world –

this is the torsion that constitutes the fold –

thus the soul is what has folds *and* is full of folds –

in order that the virtual be incarnate –

(thus the soul is what has folds and is full of folds) –

(the fold moves from inflection to inclusion) –

(infinite seriality may be the soul) –
(curvatures may be in it –)

why would something be folded, if it were
not to be enveloped, wrapped, or put into
something else? –

does what is folded exist only
in something that envelops it? –

is it not exactly point-of-view that includes? –

and when inclusion is accomplished, is it not done
                                        so continuously
it includes the sense of a finished act that is not the site,
not the place, not the point-of-view,

but what remains in point-of-view,

what *occupies* point-of-view –

necessarily a soul, a subject –

a power of envelopment *and* development,

folding when enveloped, unfolding when developed –

an implication, an explication, a complication –

a sort of city —

the course of a given street and that of another —

an infinite series of curvatures, of inflections —

the entire world enclosed in the soul by point-of-view —

Is something else needed?

Is a realization in matter also required?

We cannot be sure.

The soul has no windows by which anything
could come in or go out. It has no opening. It has no doorway.

Everything is drawn out of it, nothing comes in.

It is a cell. It resembles a sacristy more than an atom.

All activity takes place on the inside.

An inside without an outside.

We decorate the inner walls.

As its correlative, think of the independence of the facade.

The facade is riddled with holes, although there is no void

(a hole being only the site of a more rarefied matter) —

℘

Come now, let us go.

How the Body Fits on the Cross

For a while I have been watching the shadow
try to fit itself onto its tree.
The slightest wind makes it throb.
I feel my lips on my face, so obedient.
Time, says the hum in the breeze, is a verge — A what? I say.
A pang. A peck. A ridge . . .
A snail on the lowest limb of the tree
                    twistingly
follows the shade.
Up, up — voice stuck to its call — dearest accompanist,
most chastising song.
My lips move with the snail, one lick up
the trunk — joy and torture wild in the highest branches, way up,
leavening — the sun always all over them as they
crinoline-around following every
commandment, advancing each year further
into illustration, the whole head slapping as if in answer
to whatever hurried question the wind just asked,
beseeching a bit in the uppermost limbs,
invisible amnesiac, betraying like a madman —
a madman thinking he has countless friends — see how they
dance for him —
he wants banners — they banner —
he wants hot lips in conversation, quick,
see them converse — jump, turn —
the heart of this is guilty work —
the wind's desire is sharper than a scythe
and more forgetful — even more! —
it chattering again now, look — all the head radiant — the shadow
                              still crawling
                              as the one god
makes it crawl, minute by minute — (not like

the lips, not like the fast translations of the heady top) –
and how it cannot sink into the ground it lies upon,
cannot sink and stop,
hearing nothing of the leaves' rushings,
nothing of history's winnowing of the tops of
                                                things
from the dark underneathly postponements
where action slips back through the gaps in the story, the rips,
and is let to sink sootishly back down,
slack and free of purpose,
to where many deeds are hidden, the stopping place, mightily dark –
up above the sun the leaves the antennae the changes –
while here the shadow so delicately crosses
the spot where a pecking hungry-one has found, in the rip,
a little fuel, bright, quick, like the slenderness of the tune
overheard by the prisoner
as someone singing passes by
then stops to look at something and forgets
to keep the song alive – that prisoner so still –
something like madness flapping in him now
as he holds still, so still, almost not breathing, that the song
be made to start again –
Go where you like the young-looking wind hoots,
soloing into the manyness up top to see it frenzy-up –
while the shadow, approaching its tree, sluffs silkily
upon it now as, approaching zenith, sun
seizes-up things, making everything suddenly coarser –
the madman at the top
now like an argument that's increasingly
                        indefensible then finally
inaudible as the shadow
sticks itself to trunk, then ranking-limb,
then finally, lifting off-ground, is seen to rise up
alongside – then strictly *on* –
lying down over the intractable thereness of what
                                                time made –

a *shade* over a *shape* – no harvest –
a passage over a given-thing – no theft –
meaningless and still as breath intaken –
the circular day laid down upon the upthrust *given,*
the two rates of speed laid down upon each other,
almost right, the fit just-off in spots – where the limb
                              twisted,
where time twists – bad fit that the mind be made to awaken –
like the singing laying itself down over the hummed song
at the edge, always – (remember this) –
of someone's desperate listening,
one you can't possibly know is there,
behind that ordinary-looking wall,
wanting only that the singing continue,
if only for a small while longer.

In the Pasture

What am I supposed to put now
into the sea of fulfillment, the broken record of swaying
                                        plenitudes?
I press out hard
along the hurt – the campaign road – I press my thoughts, my tiny
                                                informers.
The earth curves more than I had thought
at first.
My mind, my thoughts in uniforms,
I press them out like little hieroglyphs
onto the mudslide where the clods and lips
are moving now.
Who will you be?
What will you say when it says *repeat after me*
and you can't hear it for the din
the black soil makes?
You come with your ploughshare, there, in your mouth –
it is sharp, it works for free which sharpens it, it cuts
into any distance freely thinking how good to die –
half out of their mind the words run fast and hard
over the muddy fields, seeking out boundaries
– splendid declivities.
Who will you be when it comes your turn?
When I look up I see the body of my friend climb up
                                        over the hilly rise
and redescend. There is an *other* side (my mind
knows this). I see my friend
climb down, straight down, into the open where there once
                                        was pasture.
I see the sunlight beat him down.
I see how hard it beats with its clean sticks.
I see him going in – it's *down* of course – under such

loving, into the mound it has
prepared for him, this golden freedom with its
                              filamentary
sticks.
Later, at night, the fires on the horizon-line make clear, splendidly
                                        clear, who we
must be and who (I sleep so badly now)
they are. *You have to live* something keeps whispering, by day, in
sun, under its army's yellowest of boots . . .
And you: it is so prominent the way
                    you walk
over this soil, your soil, your mind held up there
in its fiery cavity – even the day *before*
                    yesterday
still sparkling like oxygen in there – ah –
how much room you carry about in you over this field –
And tell me, did you volunteer?
Are you the last free man alive?
Are you so *full of life* – billowing dresses on the lines,
blowsy hypotheses the butterflies can make over
                        their field?
Can you pick your way among the
among? And the illustration of . . . ? And
the once-still architecture of
            the grandeur of
the sensible? the obvious? the inevitable? the true? –
the chestnut trees, the clean white napkins folded
                              under there?
the stars in the day-sky? –
the petticoat of morning-mist and the great-coat of
                              frost?
What is it my friend will have to find,
breaking down and breaking down?
The earth curves more than we had dreamed.
The slope cannot be staved against.
Rainwaters, the day-before, the syllable

that grows its root into some tiny sleeping god
and makes that great sleep shudder back
awake. The *last slaves,* when will they be alive?
The space in the heart, when
will it be planted shut, tamped-down,
choked-off with root, with growth,
that final, thirstless, silencing.
My friend is lying in the earth. No, my love is
in the earth. He's weathering, gingerly, the hurt of its
                                        downslope,
so I can't see him anymore
            from here.
Materiality has dwindled.
What is it, muddy god, that has increased
                        therefore,
according to your law?
The day before the day-before-yesterday
appears spruced-up here in my cavity, my hole,
my grandest architecture of
syllabled – form building – clean – numb-lidded
                                        gaze.
A book is lying in the dust where we last lay.
The grass is bloody under it, but that's a
whim of blood, you know, a tiny thirst.
What does Paris look like now?
The eye darkens and the great cities kneel.
The monster of the mind moves easily among its marls,
its constant inward-sucking curl –
the day is measured-out in grams of light –
the monster, measured out in grams of light,
moves gently over the playing field,
dragon of changes and adjustments,
mightiness of redefining and refinement.
I love the uniforms my thoughts are wearing.
The heels, the sleeves. The black where nothing disappears. I love

the stitching-in, each breath thread hard and tight
                              into each breath,
holding the great-coat on
that we be better-looking,
elegant informers, so well-dressed as to almost be
                              transparent.
Tender, like the pasture.
Thick and clear, like a hole that can be jumped into – oh
earth, voice, string, gardener, lens.
Hear the hard damp in these our syllables.
We dare not pray. Hear us as the cloth
the needle.
The low buzz of the trees in constant wind
terrifies.
The leader here has cheeks shaved clean
and can't misfire
because he is enslaved and as god's son
is not allowed to miss.
Someone bites his cigarette.
Someone bites hard and lets himself go,
thinking how much he'd like to measure and to draw
this hole he's forced into, how much he loves
the soil they're shoving now
– lovers of poems, of flowerings, of all misdelivered messages –
down his wide throat.

Motive Elusive

It turns out the child was not really watching
while its mother was raped. The child
was distracted. It didn't recall.
Chains were dragging over the earth.
Sleep too. Two kinds of sleep.
And the drub – as of silk – of day against light.
And the chaos of daylight up against silk –
silk warped over flesh – silk warped into sheen on the *interior latex* –
two coats of which the eyes of the child
now luster on – and the suck of such light – and the thrall
of the child notwithstanding the screaming –
and the mother, of course, suppressing the scream –
the two kinds of scream – or trying to –
and the chains still dragging over the earth –
and also scummy in spots the light on the wall,
there where it creases and corners, for example, this light,
rippling, over-reaching, the glance deft on the wall –
and the chain-link where the brain inhabits the glance –
and the push of the glance with its epic
        desire – dimpling
where the wall is pocked,
scuttling where the paint is ripped . . .
The brain climbing barehanded onto that pleating white.
The mother being slowly doled-out by the friend.
And you can't be afraid.
Where the eye is the hero.
Where the wall truly *is* a video arcade.
"Where there is personal liking, we
go": where the ground is
plural. Where there's a bony thing.
Where love won't grow.

Where the cool of the wall (where for once his small hands, un-
        impeded, can go)
feels thirsty, is sucking now, like rotting leaves,
where the palm can lie flat and feel such plenitude,
right there where the fretwork of the small screams,
like the icy breeze at the edge of the cliff,
is taken into the cool of the wall – oh don't
mistake me – the rape (ongoing) of the mother now
here in another part of the room,
late November, pipes knocking on,
is not overlooked out of simple terror
        by the child in the corner
whom Domestic Violence Services will find
tired but hopeful, reading, reading,
looking in here for where something is hiding,
thinking the light, sightseeing carefully the muffling wall –
and so on now, and long before dawn – don't frown – don't
        ask
for grief: it is a trance: the paint on the barely imagined
        ceiling
pricking at the edges till something falls down – something
infinitesimal – something the size of flaking paint
breaking loose where a body hits a wall –
a pointless loosening and then a spooring-down: white bits: almost
        soft:
which the child will notice are like the scream:
holding his free hand up to their fall:
one hand on the coolness of the wall, one reaching and pointing, then
        opening, up
to the nearly invisible toy that falls:
as if an important lid were lifting
– oh how we love the tiny things –
underneath, inside, the contents, the glance,
spinning the abundance into a fine, strong linen –
        you must

believe this – it can do – it can hold –
so that, yes, be afraid – fear the air and its steps –
fear restlessness – fear the rat –
fear life without water –
fear boundless joy – fear excellence, plenty –
fear the simplified creature – fear the flight from danger –
do not fear for the child –
propped on its hind legs,
awaiting its orphanhood –
do not fear for the child
now rising to greet its likeness on the wall,
placing its hands on the shadow's hands,
conferring wings on what it grips –
"as the air-plant does" – a true divinity –
knowing how to dive eye-first to a thing –
do not fear for the child,
its gold is hid.

Emergency

I .

Walking in the dark along the river's dark,
I can hear its small wrestling-sound,
its pasture of shutting and re-shutting pockets,
its sideways-sound and long sleek zoneless mildly-enameled
inherencies, but cannot *see* —
not even alongside — so close night's motherings — into its celluloid
untellings —
not even the slightest drifting gauzy bit of light,
folding to ripple up
the trancelike sugary vestibule
of chains and chains and chains.
Were there moon,
I'd see it climb its marble stairs
on waterfilm, I'd see
the quick secretive kneeling mists, the scalloped edgewaters,
the blossoming center-currents
that try, in their slow throat, themselves alone
to hold all still
in this — hatred, planets, broken oars —
heresies, drawn swords one wishes so one could
resheathe — face of heaven — alphabet — the center swirling on itself
as if the rest could be arrested by
sufficient urgency — *how like a heart* I think, imagining that self-insuck
from my blindness
at the rim. . . Moon, and I could see
the fine-edged slender sandbar gleam
like a raised cheekbone upon
a changing face —
I would have seen you, changing face — you,
wan homesickness, surrenderer.

I would have forgotten something.
I would have paid that dreamy attention
a woman, in a good-sized American town, alone,
late night, along a river's finery,
downriver from a power-plant,
upriver from a reservoir, is free
to pay. But it is moonless. The muscle braids-up alongside.
Cicadas churn. My wholeness now just something *alongside* –
a stammering, an unattachedness – hands in pockets – a walking straight
                                        ahead into the black,
and walking fast – as if to seed the patiently prolonging emptiness
everything not-river – everything not perfectly invisible –
seems to
possess.

2 .

The war is over says the river, *the stars are all in me.*
I peer from the bank, forgotten things seem to fly by.
There is novelty, feel its blades, says the river, rippling,
push into perdition, your fault is eternal, exciting, exciting with seeming –
the river falls over itself explaining –
why do you hurry to drown yourself in me
its flashy waves harshly laugh-up,
why do you expect constant attention,
why your eagerness for self-creation, self-explanation –
what would you explain, it weeps into its inswirls, *what would you be,* it
floats, capturing a sudden filament of gold
where someone in a house upstream turns on a light
for just a tiny while –
(the garmenture of river, the light tucked into its raveling hem) –
then it's turned off again and it's
blacker of course. *So much has passed now*
through your mind the river kissing the banks proposes.
Look away. It is best. Your post is forwardness, nothing else.
You cannot wake up. You cannot look in.

Not into here, not up, not over there, not through.
The water swirls – I can hear it – there is a bend
near here, a kind of will building,
a widening, no mud, a sifting, a clarifying –
and all of it so black, so near to me,
editing-out differences, wearing the night like a large true title,
swinging its heaviness right through appearance,
bearing the lengthening, composed entirely of minor acts,
elaborating endlessly, but without development –
why are you still here the house of cards will fall it slushes,
struggle, get up and be, climb back onto the walkway the city has provided,
the little path, good-bye, catch-up with the story, where you left off,
that is the only subject of your poem,
you have no other form but story,
and various assortments of cause and effect – publicity, existence,
how to travel faster at night –
go – repeat where was I? where was I? –
drifting thoughtfully towards common knowledge,
the war is over, the stars are in me . . .

3 ·

When she hit the child she felt something multiply.
Looking around the room everything seemed to want to be killed.
The shadows the shelves laid on the floor
were the heaviest thing she could imagine.
They clotted up in her, those grainy streaks.
She didn't know what not to do.
She turned the light off, tried to be still.
She knew if it cried again she couldn't be helped.
She tried to put herself back into herself.
She prayed to God the child not cry.
The river outside made the waiting harder.
As the dark settled, the indoors reassembled.
The lamp struck its crazed tree across the floor.
The fringes of the tasseled shade

drew stiff and powerless sentences across the wall.
She tried to hear if the baby was breathing.
She tried to put silence over what she had done.
She wanted the silence to fill the room further,
cool and wide, she wanted it
to thicken the wall between them further,
to whiten completely the present tense, to make sure her self
could be gathered up into an emptiness,
with boundaries, completely clear.
She could feel war so perfectly in her.
Not just any war but the one war
that stretches languidly from kiss to symmetry.
She could feel it grow small towns with neatly laid-out streets,
and all the new houses, privacies, fences kept up –
small gates occurred to her – she could hear hinges
and how, when people passed, one had the choice to *not look up* –
she could feel alleyways, back alleyways, and how what we call *time*
set itself down all round their secrecies
but couldn't find any way through them – how back in there
                                            were zones
where no one looked and time sat down and slept
– she felt again the *not-looking-up* –
– she felt her own name like a great fatigue –
and how in the bedroom now, with her, all over her,
the silence itself seemed like such a pity,
milking vaguely into its own eternity.
She tried to imagine the silence touching her, coating her,
                                      but it seemed
                                      too thin.

She tried to imagine it swabbing the room
but there was nowhere enough to reach
                        the corners,
nowhere enough to lap the floor –
not even half enough
to wash each spot her eye touched,
to rinse the quantities of indoor spaces now that
                              needed it

– too many rooms, too many walls and corridors,
and avenues – and streets – and silence spread so very thin –
she felt her name like a great fatigue,
how it pushed into the corners in stead of the silence,
how it washed up against the shadows with its great weight,
and how they leaned, spoorless,
onto the world that happened to be there.
She prayed to silence the child not cry.
She prayed to the wall the child not cry.

4 ·

Let us pray. *Why?* Let us pray to be a torpid river, Lord.
Why? Whom shall we compose to be the speaker
for this void? I peered over the riverbank for *you,*
to find the stars. *I* hacked out a listening
where the river grew invisible. *You* – who is that?
She turned her light on in the century of fear,
saw she was alive, saw her aliveness there
black and stunted – her aliveness like a tunnel
to the center of an earth of flesh, all flesh –
where were the beating wings, the little clouds,
where the love without beginning or end? –
let us pray, let us switch off the light and hide again,
yet further this time, from
ourselves. From *I* and *you* and *she.* Poorest devils. . . .
Nature breeds. Listen. All through the trees and grasses something ticks
at different rates, the ticking can't be represented
in the riversurface though it is
laid down upon those waters, right in there with the stars, the black-
on-black of leaves
– where the little wings? – Somewhere in the sleeve
of the greatcoat Blaise Pascal was buried in – some say it's red – his sister
sewed
the tiny piece of paper on which her brother wrote
the irrefutable proof of the existence of God –
Enjoined from reading it she did not read –

she's sewing it so carefully – she, she – the heavy fabric folded clean
over the neat thrice-folded sheet
on which his dying leans – her bent by candlelight,
the needle difficult to push through then
as it is now, each stitch hard on the thumb,
each stitch brought back and then tucked in,
that the wound in the seam be perfectly repaired,
that the break in the outline not be discerned.
Darkly sewn in. Heaven and Hell in one fold of the sleeve.
Whirling spaces all around,
though she's
bent at her task, something beating in her hands
– the little wings, where are the rustling, shifting, annunciatory wings? –
folding and unfolding in thin air could we look up? –
so that no eye can pick them out? –
him folded in the coat then lowered in,
the secret in the fold and in her hands – *not in her mind* –
his body later on dug up and not locatable
today (although the tombstone can be
visited) – Shall we pray? shall we *bend down?*
Somewhere the smell of orange rind, somewhere a cinema
shut for the night, the rows of seats in dark, the screen invisible,
what flows through it invisible, something humming in the empty hall,
some stains that can't be washed away,
some smells that grow in secret, spooring,
and words that have been pronounced in there
words that did not occupy the air, words *without breath* in them,
like the empty cup left on the table
when the last one of us finally left,
the cup which no one found for months –
and then, whose home did it turn into then? –
then history, some cities that managed not to burn,
elsewhere flames as far as the horizon,
what should the woman do
to keep herself in character
that she might love?

Easter Morning Aubade

She tried to clench the first dawnlight *inside her skull*.
Tried to feel it slather in there and make a form.
Felt the meadows the light held inside its flowing coat,
sewn into there, silkiest lining – the seams, the property-lines perfect –
and pulled them in, and laid them down along the floor of it.
There was a green hill with a thin white road, she laid that in.
There was a speckling, as where cypress have been struck, in rows,
to indicate approach, and then a temporary house – she drove those in
and laid them flat in there. She heard the word *temporary*. She felt

                        her eyes,

their tiny weights, and how there was, in fact, no glancing *out*.
Outside, further away,
the soldiers slept. Sun was beginning to graze their fingertips –
and a lance protruding, and an elbow where it rammed itself in sleep –
light pouring down the difference,
yet without waking them,
though waking up their forms.
Behind them, still misty now, the two dimensional, like a thin god, rose –
nothing could keep it – it had no feet on the ground –
a thing round which nothing could swirl,
the hooks of light unable to find hold upon its garment,
so that it could not be pulled into the furrows of the skull,
in over the rooftile that she now brought in,
and the shields which the sleepers let glide,
or the birch trees touched black at every branch on one side,
or the wire-mesh through which the *white* of five chickens hives. . . .
The intervals grow deep.
One of the soldiers rubs his face,
streamings-of-thought starting to glide all over him,
sticky frantics from the network clotting all round,
thickenings, varyings,
in which the possibility of shapeliness begins to rave,

brightening most at those edges where the skull feels itself to be
inside of something which it cannot see –
as where the lips can be felt, for instance –
and the wide light along those lips,
and the 800 mph rotational spin of the earth leaning in on them,
the interweaving of dust with nonparticulate matter, with love, with the
                                                      small stone falling
from the hand of the child leaning over the bridge down there,
up past the soldier's right shoulder, but small, because far away,
and the stone's lip as it curls the surface round it for an instant,
and the displacement of galactic matter round the orbit of the sun – is
                                                      that right? –
the child's face as the light of *effect* gathers upon it
and the stone sinks,
the thin liplike suctions of the waters closing over it,
and how to his mind it is taken in, swallowed,
how he turns to see if it will reappear on the other side or will be carried
                                                      away,
and how *forever* comes to mind, bells starting to ring in the morninglight,
and how he goes back to the place where the stone disappeared and stares
                                                      for a while,
me watching to see what will dawn on his face,
bells from three churches now across the valley, almost in synch but then
                                                      there is time,
and how as he stares I can see
that the place of disappearance has disappeared,
it cannot be recovered, his eyes darting over the moving waters,
and how a life cannot be lived therefore, as there is no place,
in which the possibility of shapeliness begins to rave,
and the soldiers awakening, of course, to the blazing *not-there,*
and the 30,000 mph of the sun's going,
rubbing its disappearance now all over this,
and the hand going back into the dirt at one's feet, fingers feeling around
for another perfect stone, wanting to see it once again, that opening.

The Turning

Sunlight bright over stone walls: houses.
Slavered into the ridged shut lids of rooftiles.
Up against their terracotta mosses: sleep and a silence
without loopholes. Birds everywhere, but still now,
$\qquad\qquad$ so invisible –
wings tucked, each body-knot furled up
$\qquad\qquad$ into the sunlight,
$\qquad\qquad$ directionless.
Whisperfree instant.
And more sun (no voices in it).
More of the faithfulness, the real.
And faithful the gaiety where sun flickers over length of wall
having crossed through boughs.
And faithful where a hammering rises – twice –
through the low-lying fog out of which the bits of
$\qquad\qquad$ hills in the valley
pronounce themselves – walled towns at the tip of each
$\qquad\qquad$ voluble
upthrusting – gleaming towns – fog in long thin

thirsty liquefactions fingering into the bottoms,

fog in the river-willows, fog tight-knitted in the hayrows and stacks,
wet on the slick bottom-grasses where in that damp
$\qquad\qquad$ the dog still sleeps.
There is a war between singular and plural.
Where in the looking the sun beats all things
$\qquad\qquad$ apart.
Where the shadows it makes meet and mingle.

The sun so poor here in its words.
Rising now without *left* and *right* along the Roman wall. Up along its
$\qquad\qquad$ ruined crenellated

rim – fragrant? fat? – and down
into the rimtop-basin rain
            over the seven
centuries has carved. . . .
There is a war.
Two parallels that will not meet have formed
a wall.
The sun revolves because of our revolving in
                            the wall.
Therefore a war. As with these words. Wall of new paper my
                    phantom-eyed need – *(that I*
should name you) – presses down on. *Change* on the wall now where
                                        a single bird
                                        inscribes its
disappearances. Gray flicked across the graynesses
                        these seams and
                        mortarings
blink forth. Bright whites and citrines
                gleaming forth,
layerings, syllables of
        the most loud
        invisible
that stick (no departure and no return) to their single
                        constantly revised
(I saw men yesterday, tuck-pointing, on their scaffold)
lecture on what
most matters: sun: now churchbells breaking up
                in twos and threes
                the flock
which works across in
            granular,
forked, suddenly cacophonic
            undulation
            (though at the level
of the inaudible) large differences of rustling, risings and lowerings,
                            swallowings of
                            silence where the wings

en masse lift off – and then the other (indecipherable) new
                              silence where
                         wings aren't
used and the flock floats in
unison –
                    a flying-in-formation sound which
I can see across the wall (as if loud) – shrapnel of
                         blacknesses
                         against the brightnesses –
fistfuls thrown (as if splattered) then growing fantastically
                              in size (also now
                              rising swiftly) as
they come – a stem of silence which blossoms suddenly
as it vanishes from the wall – (turning, the whole
                              flock
turning) – exfoliation of aural clottings where all wings open now
                                   to break
and pump – vapor of accreting inaudibles –
innermost sound scratchy with clawed and necked
                         and winged
indecipherables (a herald) – whole flock now rising highest just before it
turns to write the longest version yet against the whole
length of the wall where the churchbells
have begun to cease and
one name is called out (but low, down near the Roman
                              gate) and one
car from down there sputters
up – (the light brightest now, it almost
                    true morning) –
these walls these streets the light the shadow in them
the throat of the thing – birds reassembling over the roof
in syncopated undulations of cooing as they settle. . . .
I look down into the neighbor's garden.
The wall rises up clean, undiluted, from its bed
                              of green.
What if I could hear the sound of petals falling
                    off the head that
                    holds them

when it's time?
What if I could hear where something is suddenly
                                        complete?
The pinetree marionette-like against the wall – but still,
                                        unused.
Whose turn is it now? Whose?

Recovered from the Storm

I went out afterwards to see.
Wide silvery hypotheses of memorizing waters.
In them – so deeply – the incomplete pictures.
Twigs, seeds, nuts, limbs scattered over the streets,
distemper's trophies gathering round our footfalls.
I looked at them carefully, wide awake in that monologue.
Some branches thrown down in the middle of things.
Cars not yet venturing. Dusk so blue in its black.
And whole bushes torn from some too-thin origin.
And drowned heads of things strewn wildly through
our singular, tender, green,
          clarifications. . .
Am I supposed to put them back together –
these limbs, their leaves, the tiny suctioned twig-end joints – ?
these branches shoved deep into my silky glance – ?
these maples' outtakes streaked over the lawn – their thorns, their blithe
footnotes . . . ? And the trellis cracked from the weight of the freefall?
And the boxelder standing like an overburdened juggler –
so laden now he cannot remember
the sugary spinnings, the bright fingerings of . . .
Oh limpid puddles with your ditties of fate . . .
There's a shovel by the window.
There's contagion by the gutter.
There's a cartoon upstairs where the children are hidden.
So this is the wingbeat of the underneathly, ticking –
this iridescent brokenness, this wet stunted nothingness –
busy with its hollows – browsing abstractly with its catastrophic wingtips
the tops of our world, ripping pleatings of molecule,
unjoining the slantings, the slippery wrinklings we don't even grasp
          the icily free *made-nature* of yet?
Why are we here in this silly moonlight?
What is the mind meant to tender among splinters?

What was it, exactly, was meant to be *shored?*
Whose dolled-up sorceries *against confusion* now?
The children are upstairs, we will keep them tucked in –
as long as we can, as long as you'll let us.
I hear your pitch. How containment is coughing,
under the leafbits, against the asphalt.
How the new piles of kindling are mossily giggling
     their kerosene cadenza
all long the block in the riddled updrafts.
I pick up and drag one large limb from the path.

Of the Ever-Changing Agitation in the Air

The man held his hands to his heart as he danced.
He slacked and swirled.
The doorways of the little city
blurred. Something
leaked out,
kindling the doorframes up,
making each entranceway
less true.
And darkness gathered
although it does not fall. . . . And the little dance,
swinging this human all down the alleyway,
nervous little theme pushing itself along,
braiding, rehearsing,
constantly incomplete so turning and tacking –
oh what is there to finish? – his robes made rustic by the reddish swirl,
which grows darker towards the end of the avenue of course,
one hand on his chest,
one flung out to the side as he dances, taps, sings,
on his scuttling toes, now humming a little,
now closing his eyes as he twirls, growing smaller,
why does the sun rise? remember me always dear for I will
return –
liberty spooring in the evening air,
into which the lilacs open, the skirts uplift,
liberty and the blood-eye careening gently over the giant earth,
and the cat in the doorway who does not mistake the world,
eyeing the spots where the birds must eventually land –

The Guardian Angel of the Little Utopia: five lines from the end, the line is from Henry Vaughan's "Distraction."

Little Requiem: asked to write on Anna Ahkmatova, I turned to the famous "Requiem" she wrote, at different intervals, concerning the arrests and incarcerations of her son. The image of him "being led away" appears in that poem.

Flood takes lines 261-304 of Ovid's "Metamorphoses" – the short section titled "The Flood" in the Humphries translation – and involves itself with the events it describes by other means.

Oblivion Aubade: in both this poem, and in *Sea-Blue Aubade*, the references at the very end are to the Odysseus story – here, in particular, to his being first recognized, upon homecoming, by his dog. Lines 6 and 7 are from Wallace Stevens.

Which but for Vacancy: "a cracked pod calls" is Theodore Roethke's phrase. Looking "gigantically down" is from Edgar Allen Poe.

That Greater Than Which Nothing: near the end, the phrase "it's the light, you can't keep it out" is from Charles Wright's poem "Virgo Descending."

The End of Progress Aubade: line 17 refers to Samuel Coleridge's image, in his poem " The Aeolian Harp," of the act of imagination as a wind "playing" such an instrument. "Clevedon, Somersetshire" is the place where the poem was composed.

The Hurrying-Home Aubade uses, in most of the lines marked off by quotation marks, Ovid's telling of the Orpheus and Eurydice myth (in the Humphries translation). Near the very end, though, the line "and under their tongues are mischief" is the Psalmist's.

Le Manteau de Pascal: all the "Manteau" poems are loosely inspired by the Magritte painting of Pascal's coat. One presumes it represents the coat in which Pascal was buried, and in whose hem or sleeve or "fold" the note containing the "irrefutable proof of the existence of God" is said to have been stitched, at his request, unread, by his sister, upon his death. The section dated "July 11" is a fragment from Hopkins' journals. In section 13 the quotations are from Magritte's notebooks. The poem is dedicated to Ann Carson, whose work inspired it.

The Shadow of Peter is said to have healed all those it grazed as he passed by.

The Guardian Angel of Point of View: the first three lines use an image, and phrasing, from Rilke's "Uncollected Poems."

The Guardian Angel of the Swarm (another "Manteau" poem) is a conversation with Gilles Deleuze's *"The Fold"* – a study of Leibnitz and the Baroque. It uses fragments of his argument – often rewritten – to review, and in spots to argue with, his brilliant intuitions.

In The Pasture: the emotion, in this poem, is born, in part, out of reading Mandelstam's "Voronezh Notebooks" in the Richard and Elizabeth McKane translation. The poem is an elegy for a loved one.

Motive Elusive: the two fragments in quotation marks are from Marianne Moore.

Emergency: Emmanuel Levinas' thinking figures, for me, in the dynamic of this poem, as well as in "The Guardian Angel of the Corridor" – exemplified, perhaps, by these remarks (from *Existence and Existents*): "What is absolute in the relationship between existence and an existent, in an instant, consists in the mastery the existent exercises on existence, but also in the weight of existence on the existent . . . In the *fatigue* of the subject inescapably burdened with itself, weighed down by its own materiality."

Easter Morning Aubade: there is no need to recognize Piero della Francesca's "Resurrection" here, but it provides this particular rendition of the sleep of the soldiers at Christ's grave. Near the end, the phrase "forever comes to mind" is from an early poem by James Galvin.

The notion of *errancy* is wonderfully touched upon in this passage from Linda Gregerson's *The Reformation of the Subject* (Chapter 3): "Epic action begins with a gaze in the mirror. When Spenser thematizes the gaze, he inscribes Eros as a species of reformed narcissism, the closed embrace broken to allow for the discursive path of knightly "error," or wandering. Other critics have noted how vividly etymology appears to structure Spenser's poem: "discourse" derives from *discurrere* (to run back and forth) as "error" or errancy derives from *errare* (to wander). . . . Knightly errancy begins with a gaze . . . "

ABOUT THE AUTHOR

JORIE GRAHAM has received numerous awards for her work, including the 1996 Pulitzer Prize in poetry for *The Dream of the Unified Field: Selected Poems 1974-1994.* She lives in Cambridge, Massachusetts, and teaches at Harvard University.